29 DAYS TO DIFFERENT: LOVE

MIKE NAPPA

AspirePress

29 Days to Different: Love
© 2021 Nappaland Communications Inc.
Published by Aspire Press
An imprint of Hendrickson Publishing Group
Rose Publishing, LLC
P.O. Box 3473
Peabody, Massachusetts 01961-3473 USA
www.HendricksonPublishingGroup.com

ISBN: 978-1-62862-923-1

Unless otherwise indicated, all Scripture quotations are taken from the Holy Bible, New Living Translation, copyright © 1996, 2004, 2015 by Tyndale House Foundation. Used by permission of Tyndale House Publishers, a Division of Tyndale House Ministries, Carol Stream, Illinois 60188. All rights reserved.

Scripture quotations marked (NIV) are taken from the Holy Bible, New International Version®, NIV®. Copyright © 1973, 1978, 1984, 2011 by Biblica, Inc.™ Used by permission of Zondervan. All rights reserved worldwide. www.zondervan.com. The "NIV" and "New International Version" are trademarks registered in the United States Patent and Trademark Office by Biblica, Inc.™

Scripture quotations marked (KJV) are taken from the King James Version of the Bible.

Printed in the United States of America
011120VP

"But the Holy Spirit produces this kind of fruit in our lives: love, joy, peace, patience, kindness, goodness, faithfulness, gentleness, and self-control.
There is no law against these things!"

—GALATIANS 5:22–23

CONTENTS

Now What?...96

The Most Important Parts.............................131

INTRODUCTION
WHAT IS 29 DAYS TO DIFFERENT?

Welcome!

I'm glad to meet you because, if you're reading this book, it means you have a desire to be changed spiritually—to cultivate habits over the next 29 days that'll allow the fruit of Christ's Spirit to grow in you and move you toward spiritual maturity. I want that for you too, so we're already on the same page (literally).

But before we get started, I must be the bearer of bad news:

You are incapable of creating any spiritually significant change in yourself.

Sure, you can look good, act well, and even train your mind to think in ways that fill you with satisfaction at your human efforts for self-improvement . . .

Ah, but that's the problem, isn't it?

No matter how strongly you exercise your will, no matter what *you* do, it's still a human effort. Every attempt you make to better yourself, to live holy, or to produce good fruit will always be tainted by the ever-present human disease: *sin.* As the Scriptures tell us:

> All of us, like sheep, have strayed away. We have left God's paths to follow our own. —ISAIAH 53:6

The LORD looks down from heaven on the entire human race; he looks to see if anyone is truly wise, if anyone seeks God. But no, all have turned away; all have become corrupt. No one does good, not a single one! —PSALM 14:2–3

For everyone has sinned; we all fall short of God's glorious standard. —ROMANS 3:23

And what's worse, we're not only infected with sin, we are overcome by it. It's so ingrained in the way we think and act and believe that Jesus had to tell us plainly: "Everyone who sins is a slave of sin" (John 8:34). So this is our bad news: We may long sincerely to be the finest examples of Christ followers, but the truth is that we're slaves to sin, incapable of creating that authentic change we so desperately desire in ourselves.

This truth can feel very heavy—and many people are already painfully aware of their faults and their powerlessness to change themselves. Instead of getting trapped under that weight, let's look forward, because in spite of the bad news . . .

There is still good news:
We don't have to change ourselves.
Again, the promise of Jesus is clear:

"Remain in me, and I will remain in you. For a branch cannot produce fruit if it is severed from the vine, and you cannot be fruitful unless you remain in me. Yes, I am the vine; you are the branches. *Those who remain in me, and I in them, will produce much fruit.* For apart from me you can do nothing." —JOHN 15:4–5 (emphasis mine)

An old pastor friend frequently explained this concept in this way:

Mikey, he'd say, *go into my backyard and sit under that apple tree. And listen, just listen. If you're very quiet, you'll hear that tree begin to grunt and groan and strain. After much effort and toil, that old tree of will pop out an apple on the branch, right before your very eyes.*

Then, with a twinkle in his eyes, Kent would pat me wisely on the shoulder and wait, because we all know that, without a doubt, *that's* how fruit grows . . . right?

Of course not!

And that was my mentor's point. Fruit doesn't grow because a tree puts forth great effort to bring about change. Fruit grows on trees because *that's what fruit trees do when they're healthy* . . . when their roots go deep and they're nourished by sunshine and water and soil. The fruit tree doesn't pop out apples as an act of its will. It simply cooperates with the Life that surrounds, fills, and feeds it. And then, in the fullness of time, that dependent cooperation with God produces fruit.

This principle also applies to how we develop the fruit of the Spirit.

The *fruit* of the Spirit flows naturally from being spiritually tethered to—and dependent upon—Jesus, our only authentic "Vine."

So, the best way to help you create habits to cultivate spiritual growth and *produce good fruit* in your daily life is to point you to Jesus. Every day. For 29 days.

That's what *29 Days to Different* is about. You'll notice this is not your typical devotional book, nor your ordinary Bible study resource. Instead, each week follows a pattern:

- DAY 1: The Week's Scripture
- DAY 2: Devotion
- DAY 3: Imagination Exercise
- DAY 4: Exploratory Essay
- DAY 5: Devotion
- DAY 6: Emotion Exercise
- DAY 7: Comfort-Zone Challenge

The format of each day varies, but here's the one promise I make to you: For the next four weeks (plus one day!) we'll take the first-listed quality from the classic "Fruit of the Spirit" Scripture in Galatians 5:22–23 and, with that quality in mind, we will point ourselves repeatedly, relentlessly, habitually toward Jesus, our Vine.

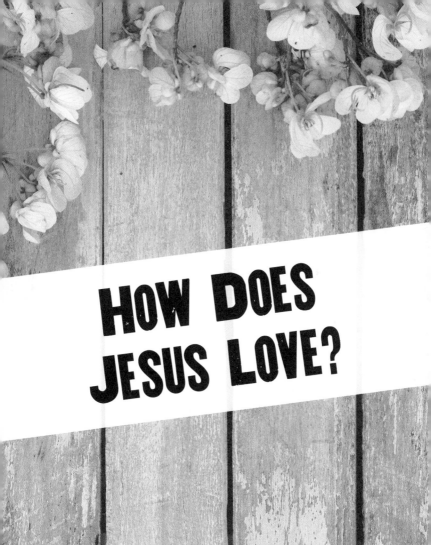

HOW DOES
JESUS LOVE?

JESUS . . . THEN

Jesus returned to the Mount of Olives, but early the next morning he was back again at the Temple. A crowd soon gathered, and he sat down and taught them. As he was speaking, the teachers of religious law and the Pharisees brought a woman who had been caught in the act of adultery. They put her in front of the crowd.

"Teacher," they said to Jesus, "this woman was caught in the act of adultery. The law of Moses says to stone her. What do you say?"

They were trying to trap him into saying something they could use against him, but Jesus stooped down and wrote in the dust with his finger. They kept demanding an answer, so he stood up again and said, "All right, but let the one who has never sinned throw the first stone!" Then he stooped down again and wrote in the dust.

When the accusers heard this, they slipped away one by one, beginning with the oldest, until only Jesus was left in the middle of the crowd with the woman. Then Jesus stood up again and said to the woman, "Where are your accusers? Didn't even one of them condemn you?"

"No, Lord," she said.

And Jesus said, "Neither do I. Go and sin no more."

— JOHN 8:1–11

U se this space to journal your thoughts and prayers about what you've read today. Feel free to use the questions below as prompts, or write whatever else is on your mind.

1. As you read John 8:1–11, what's the "big question" that comes to your mind?

2. What do you suspect the answer to that question is?

3. Imagine a world in which Jesus throws the first stone in the execution of this woman. How does that change your life yesterday, today, and tomorrow?

4. What would you like to say to Jesus after reading John 8:1–11? Write it out as a prayer.

THE BIG QUESTION

The Holy Spirit produces this kind of fruit in our lives: love . . .

— GALATIANS 5:22

It can be interesting to read a passage of Scripture until it raises a question in your mind, and then to reread that same passage with that question in mind. For instance, looking at John 8:1–11 yesterday, the big question that came to me was:

Why aren't we allowed to see the whole picture of this moment?

I want it to be like one of those NFL "True View" replay videos where they start the play, then freeze the scene while the camera zips around to capture the field from all angles. *Swooosh*—we zoom in for a closer look at the angry postures of the woman's accusers. *Swiiish*—we spin 180 degrees and get a close-up of the exact moment when Jesus stoops down with his finger pointing at the ground. *Sszzpow*—we rocket back at dizzying speed to view the expression on the sinful woman's face just before we zoom out again and then fast-forward to the end of the action.

But the gospel writer doesn't give us anything like that. So we're left reading this abbreviated scene, asking questions like: If this sinful woman was actually "caught in the act of adultery," where is her equally guilty, now-invisible partner? Was adultery, for her, an act of love, or simply a business transaction—or perhaps something worse? In her public humiliation, did her enemies bother to clothe her after tearing her from the bed (or wherever they found her)? Or did they parade her naked through the streets as was a common practice of their Roman conquerors—and if so, was that perhaps why Jesus turned his gaze away from her shame?

And WHAT in the world was Jesus doing with that whole writing-in-the-dust thing?

There's so much here that we can't see, that we want to see, that—dare I say it?—God himself has prevented us from seeing, or at least from seeing with certainty.

Now why would God do that to me, and to you, and to all of those in history who have read John 8:1–11? I don't have a complete answer to that question. But I do have a sneaking suspicion. See, there is one thing prominently on display, spectacularly made known in the details of this moment of John's gospel:

Christ loves a sinner.

And maybe that's why all that other stuff was unnecessary and left out of this gospel account. Maybe John, the writer, and God, the Author, wanted us to see what was really important amid all the self-righteous shouting and titillation and teasing of bloody violence.

Jesus loves sinners, John tells us, and this woman right here—she is proof. Now that we know that, now that we've seen it with our own eyes in the pages of Scripture, only one question remains:

What are we going to do with a love like that?

DAY 3

WINDOW-PAINTING

> Then Jesus stood up again and said to the woman, "Where are your accusers? Didn't even one of them condemn you?"
>
> "No, Lord," she said.
>
> And Jesus said, "Neither do I. Go and sin no more."
>
> — JOHN 8:10–11

Open the curtains on a large window in your home. Go ahead, I'll wait. Now stick with me on this: Imagine that window is a canvas on which your mind can paint anything it can dream.

First, in the top left corner, choose a thin imaginary brush, and use your finest lettering to scrawl the words of John 8:10–11 there. What artistic flourishes will you include? Which words will you highlight in color or size? Why?

Next, take measure of the rest of the space left on your window-canvas. Now you can do more detailed work, painting the full scene of John 8:10–11 in your mind's eye.

18

No, no, don't just splash the watercolors (or oils, or acrylics, or whatever your mind is using today) onto the pane. Let's plan this out a bit first. Take as much time as you need, and feel free to write out your thoughts in the margins on this page. Here we go:

- What belongs in the center of your painting?

- Where does the light come from? What's in shadow?

- How will you place the elements of the moment? Which parts of the scene are facing the viewer, and which are turned away? What's in the foreground, what's in the back?

- What color is the sky? The ground? The skin of the ruddy-cheeked adulterer?

- Whose eyes will make your viewer linger?

- Who is clean, who is dirty; who is rich or poor?

- What forms the background expanse, and just how does it frame the scene?

- What kinds of texture will you create beneath the colors you share?

- In your mind, what will you do that makes this painting a true work of art?

Ah, very good. I had no idea you'd be this skilled. Nice work. Now, pause to form the full painting in your mind, attaching each layer to your window, brushing on each element as it seems best to you.

You have just painted a clarion moment in history upon the retina of your mind's eye. Look closely at this invisible work of art. It is a private thing, an intimate thing, a gift that God has given exclusively to you.

What do you see here, in your lushly painted windowpane?

What does it say to you about the way that Jesus loves the sinner?

Write your thoughts in the space below, then repeat them as a prayer to Christ who loves you.

LOVE WORDS

> As he was speaking, the teachers of religious law and the Pharisees brought a woman who had been caught in the act of adultery. They put her in front of the crowd.
>
> "Teacher," they said to Jesus, "this woman was caught in the act of adultery. The law of Moses says to stone her. What do you say?"
>
> — JOHN 8:3–5

It can be difficult at times to reconcile the idea that the God of Moses and the Christ of our New Testament are one and the same. Yet Jesus himself made it clear that was the case.

"The Father and I are one," he said to his disciples (John 10:30). "Anyone who has seen me has seen the Father!" he told Philip (John 14:9). And, believe it or not, during his famous Sermon on the Mount, Christ even told everyone, "Don't misunderstand why I have come. I did not come to abolish the law of Moses or the writings of the prophets. No, I came to accomplish their purpose" (Matthew 5:17).

"The law of Moses says to stone her," the teachers and Pharisees said in John 8:5. The code to which they referred is found in a few places in the Old Testament; one example is from Deuteronomy 22:22: "If a man is discovered committing adultery, both he and *the woman must die.* In this way, you will purge Israel of such evil" (emphasis mine).

So yes, the teachers and Pharisees were right. Killing this woman would appear to be exactly the condemnation of sin that God both wanted and demanded, a penalty practiced for thousands of years.

So how does this happen? How is it that first God tells Moses, "the woman must die," but then Jesus, God-in-bones, tells this adulterous woman, "Didn't even one of them condemn you? . . . Neither do I."

How can this be the self-same Person? How can the One be both judge and emancipator for the identical offense?

The would-be lawyer in me argues that God created the rule and thus, as its sole Creator, he alone holds the legal authority to create the exception to the rule. That might've been what Jesus did here—but I don't think any argument that places God in the defendant's seat really delivers a full answer. And I'm not sure anyone can answer this question fully on this side of heaven. So let me just offer my opinion, and then you can make an opinion of your own.

I think the reason lies in what we don't know about a single word:

LOVE

First John 4:8 reminds us that "God is love." If this is true, then love can't be neatly defined, because God himself is indefinable. We can't know him in his entirety because of his inherent limitlessness and our shockingly limited comprehension. As Paul said, "Now we see things imperfectly, like puzzling reflections in a mirror" (1 Corinthians 13:12).

And even the word itself, "love," seems indefinable. After all, our English language has dozens of terms to communicate "love"—all of which imbue a slightly different meaning on the actual definition of love. Even the ancient Greek that was used in Christ's time had at least four variations of meaning on the term.

Still, we can know one thing with certainty:

God is love.

What this tells me is that love, like God, encompasses more words and shades and layers of meaning than we can fully understand.

So, when God stood before Moses and said, "the [adulterous] woman must die," he spoke judgment based in love for his people—desiring the best for the object of his love (the nation of Israel). And when God stood before the adulterous woman and told her, "Neither do I [condemn you]," he spoke mercy based in love for one woman—desiring to cancel punishment for the object of his love, even after she'd chosen so much less than God's best.

Love, it seems then, must contain some element of both judgment (desiring the best) and mercy (hope for even the worst). Judgment and mercy holding hands are somehow components of the same indescribable love Christ has for sinners. And maybe that's why the sons of Korah could write in Psalm 85:10 (KJV), "Mercy and truth are met together; righteousness and peace have kissed each other."

Now it's time for you to weigh in.

Look again at the account of the woman caught in adultery in John 8:1–11. You see the word "love" on display in the person of Jesus, no?

Now look closer.

What other words and phrases, what other elements and layers of love describe the Son of God in this moment? *Unwavering*, perhaps. *Protective*, maybe. And the rest? Well, that's up to you to decide.

See if you can fill this space with all the words and phrases that God brings to your mind. Let the prayer that follows be an honest expression of your love in return.

IN PERSON

Jesus returned to the Mount of Olives, but early the next morning he was back again at the Temple. A crowd soon gathered, and he sat down and taught them.

—JOHN 8:1–2

When we think about the question, "How does Jesus love?" it's easy to overlook the first and most obvious answer:

In person.

Have you wondered how Christianity would be different if Christ hadn't made himself accessible to people? If, instead of going out to public gathering spaces, he'd hidden himself away and given only obscure clues as to his whereabouts?

My freshman year of college I heard of a secret organization on campus. They met, the chalked message on the sidewalk said, in some indecipherable location at "half past the milking hour." I imagine they had fun with their secret club, but for those of us on the outside they were less than irrelevant. Just some nobodies who sometimes wrote silly messages on the sidewalks.

What if Christ had been like that, hidden away and unwilling to meet actual people? Disconnected from those he'd come to seek and to save (Luke 19:10), disassociated from those who needed protection from the Pharisees' systematized, dangerously zealous, religious indifference? Where would God be found if he'd been unwilling to meet us in person? Because, let's face it, if God wanted to hide, none of us—not the most holy or the cleverest—would ever be able to locate him.

I heard a story once—I'm told it was true—of two men hunting for God in a South American forest. Everywhere they went, they called out for him. One dug a six-foot hole and cried, "God, God, come out of the hole." Another climbed a tree and called to the wind, "God, God, come from the horizon!" And finally God placed a missionary in that forest who heard them calling. Through that missionary, those two men heard of Jesus for the first time—in person, for themselves.[1]

What if Christ had demanded that kind of haphazard search of everyone who wanted to find him? If every day was a brutal, never-ending game of hide-and-seek with his followers? "Jesus, Jesus! Are you in that marketplace?" "Jesus, Jesus! Are you hiding in that boat?" "Jesus, Jesus! Do you despise me so much that you must keep yourself a secret from me unless I desperately, accidentally stumble upon you?" But he is not like that, as John recorded in his gospel:

> Early the next morning he was back again at the
> Temple. A crowd soon gathered, and he sat down . . .

Do you know why the Pharisees and the distraught, adulterous woman were able to find Christ so easily when they wanted him? Because Jesus was "back again at the Temple." Because he deliberately placed himself nearby—and he did it so often that people learned to expect it. Because he opened himself to anyone—friend or foe, righteous and sinner, rich and poor—who wanted to know him. He came "back again" time after time, making himself predictable, accessible, available.

What do you call someone who loves like that?

Well, John gave us a hint when he recorded Jesus saying, "I no longer call you slaves, because a master doesn't confide in his slaves. Now you are *my friends*" (John 15:15, emphasis mine).

Take a minute to think about your best friend. I'll go first: When everything was lost, when death was at my door, I called Kevin. I didn't worry about whether he'd be there, or even if he'd respond. I just said, "Kevin, I need you." And he was there, beginning to end, and then after the end, and through the worst and on to more. And though he lives far away, he's still near me, ready to respond anytime I ask. Why? Because Kevin is my *friend*. I know where to find him, and I know he will help me because Kevin learned friendship first from Jesus, and now he shares that same kind of friendship with me.

Still, in my darker moments I ask myself: What if Jesus had been the kind of person who liked to hide, who avoided the unwashed crowds, who didn't want to deal with confrontation or religious zealots or mix with relentless sinners? What if instead of saying, "Come to me, all of you who are weary and carry heavy burdens" (Matthew 11:28), he'd said, "Come to me, only a few of you who are smart and funny, and can carry my bags for me . . ."?

Then I realize that, like a meeting at "half past the milking hour," the answer to that question is irrelevant. Because Jesus is not at all like that.

Christ is the One who intentionally blew past formalities. He is our God who became literally and humiliatingly a "Son of Man"—and the Savior who went early in the morning to sit in a public place where any and all could find him. Although his physical body is not with us today, he is still present with us, constantly available and accessible to us though his Holy Spirit.

So instead of asking "Where has Jesus hidden today?" we can gaze directly at him (in Scripture) and ask, "How does Jesus love today?" When I consider that question, the first and most obvious answer remains:

In person.

U se this page to journal your thoughts and prayers about what you've read today. Feel free to use the questions below as prompts, or write whatever else is on your mind.

1. If Jesus loves in person, what do you think that meant for the people who lived when he was on earth? Describe it in your own words.

2. Why is it important that Jesus demonstrated his love in person instead of from a distance?

3. Christ's Holy Spirit communicates Jesus' "in person" love nowadays. What does that say to you about how Jesus loves? Write it out as a prayer.

MUCH LOVE

> The teachers of religious law and the Pharisees
> brought a woman who had been caught in the act
> of adultery. They put her in front of the crowd.
>
> — JOHN 8:3

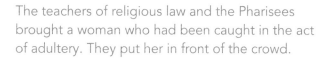

It's time for us to move past reading about the nameless woman caught in adultery and begin to know her. Be warned, this will be a bit uncomfortable. (If it's not, then do it again until it is.)

First, take a moment to remember the most humiliating moment in your life. No, I'm not talking about that time you dreamed you were speaking to a large crowd and discovered you'd forgotten your pants. I'm talking about that other time, the one that really happened, the one that left you feeling small, vulnerable, and powerless to do anything but suffer the embarrassment you felt.

Ah, now you're remembering it. It's likely your stomach has clenched slightly, maybe your brow has furrowed and your armpits have become damp. It's a memory you don't want to keep, but today at least, it's important to live that moment again. See it in your mind; hear it in your ears; taste again that awful instant of unavoidable shame.

There's no need to write it down. Just remember that humiliation until it is a familiar pain again.

I'm sorry you suffered that indignity. But take heart— today God is going to use that memory for good.

Now, with your humiliation in mind, think of something that could symbolize that experience—something that would have meaning for you and only you. Sketch it in the blank space below.

As you look at your sketch, think of the words that you associate with that symbol. Shame, perhaps? Anger? Sorrow and fear? Helplessness? What other words begin to populate your thoughts?

I want you to *feel* this moment again, feel it now, distinctly, because the sympathetic pain you still feel for Former-You can stand in—at least in part—for the horror and hopelessness experienced by the nameless woman of John 8.

Look at her again, this time from inside her skin instead of from the outside. She is shockingly "caught in the act of adultery," fully exposed, harassed, humiliated, and paraded through town. And then her would-be murderers "put her in front of the crowd"—gleeful at their ability to set her on degrading display before everyone. Then she's forced into the defendant's seat at a sham trial, already condemned, forbidden to speak on her own behalf, her life in the hands of a rabbi she's never met.

How small she must have felt. How used. How many regrets must've weighed on her soul.

Now, Rabbi Jesus looks at her—looks at you—looks at the symbols of humiliation that both of you carry. And simply blows them away like fingerprints in the dust.

Luke 7:36–50 records another encounter Jesus had with a "sinful woman." Their stories have similarities. Jesus said of that other woman: "I tell you, her sins—and they are many— have been forgiven, so she has shown me much love. But a person who is forgiven little shows only little love" (Luke 7:46).

Much love.

Look again at that symbol of shame you sketched above. Think again of these two women. It's possible that your humiliations could lead to only pain, judgment, and death. But then Christ makes things messy, doesn't he? Bringing his love to bear on the situation, he causes something unexpected to happen. He takes those women's shame— yours too—and turns it into pure gratefulness. It's a seed planted in the soul that grows into something not there before, something that contains his own DNA inside it, good fruit that will last forever:

Much love.

WHERE THE CROWD GATHERS

A crowd soon gathered, and he sat down . . .

— JOHN 8:2

All right. You're ready.

You and I have talked for almost a week, seeking answers to the question, "How does Jesus love?" It's time now to get outside of your comfort zone, to stretch your boundaries and get beyond your isolated little bubble . . . to sit down where the crowd gathers.

So this is your calling for today: Go someplace public—a coffee house, or a local shopping center, maybe even a park if the weather's nice, or a café where you can carry on a conversation with the waitress and people at tables nearby. Carry a notepad and a pen with you.

Bring a friend for moral support if you like.

Pretend you're a journalist researching a story. Summon your courage, stop at least two people, and ask them this question:

"In your opinion, how does Jesus love?"

If it helps you, bring this book along and tell people I've put you up to this, that it's an experiment to discover what people think about how Jesus loves.

Then let your subjects define what aspect of that question they'll answer. Some will say, "Do you mean this? Or do you mean that?" Tell them whatever they want the question to mean is what you want. Try to avoid putting answers in their mouths, or even speaking too much.

And then listen. Take notes. Nod and be interested in what your subjects have to say. Ask people to explain what they mean. Don't correct them, don't tell them, "Well, really this is the way it is . . ." Just pay attention, and be available.

You see, the real experiment here is not what their answers will be. It is to see if you might hear a whisper of God today, if you might catch a glimpse of Christ's love constantly at work in the greater world around you. I think you may be surprised by what you find. And if not, well, at least you got out of the house, right?

When you're finished, come back here and write your thoughts about the experience in the space provided. Let those thoughts become a prayer for you, a moment of conversation between you and God to end your day.

_ _

_ _

_ _

_ _

_ _

_ _

_ _

_ _

_ _

_ _

P.S. If the thought of talking to strangers has you hyperventilating and seeing blue dots at the edges of your vision, you can post the question on social media instead, or email it to people you know. But if you're willing to risk getting out into the world to pose this question, I think you just might enjoy yourself!

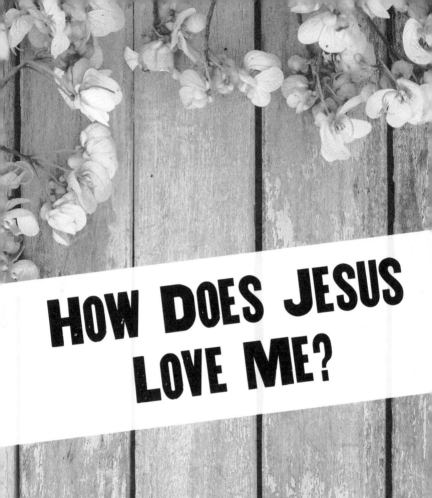

HOW DOES JESUS LOVE ME?

JESUS . . . NOW

See how very much our Father loves us, for he calls us his children, and that is what we are! —1 JOHN 3:1

We know what real love is because Jesus gave up his life for us. —1 JOHN 3:16

And this hope will not lead to disappointment. For we know how dearly God loves us, because he has given us the Holy Spirit to fill our hearts with his love. —ROMANS 5:5

And I am convinced that nothing can ever separate us from God's love. Neither death nor life, neither angels nor demons, neither our fears for today nor our worries about tomorrow—not even the powers of hell can separate us from God's love. No power in the sky above or in the earth below—indeed, nothing in all creation will ever be able to separate us from the love of God that is revealed in Christ Jesus our Lord. —ROMANS 8:38–39

Love is patient, love is kind.

*It does not envy, it does not boast,
it is not proud.*

*It does not dishonor others,
it is not self-seeking,
it is not easily angered,
it keeps no record of wrongs.*

*Love does not delight in evil
but rejoices with the truth.*

*It always protects, always trusts,
always hopes, always perseveres.*

Love never fails.

—1 CORINTHIANS 13:4–8 (NIV)

Use this page to journal your thoughts and prayers about what you've read today. Feel free to follow one or both of the prompts below, or write whatever else is on your mind.

1. Write a letter to the 10-year-old version of you. What would you like that child to understand about the Scriptures you read today?

2. Write a letter to be read on your birthday 10 years from now. What do you want that older version of you to remember about the Scriptures you read today?

ONE FOR THE HISTORY BOOKS

Love is patient, love is kind.

— 1 CORINTHIANS 13:4 (NIV)

There is a moment in Mark's gospel when a blind man causes a commotion in an effort to gain Jesus' attention. You can read the full account in Mark 10:46–52, but suffice it to say that the blind man was more than annoying. So annoying, in fact, that people in the crowd yelled for him to shut up and quit bothering everybody.

You've probably been in a similar situation, right? I picture it almost like the ubiquitous drunk in the stadium at a football game who won't stop yelling at the refs or shouting inane trash talk at the sidelines. Or maybe it's like when a celebrity is accosted by the paparazzi, everyone shouting "Look here! Look over here!" until all that noise just kind of buzzes together into one loud, narcissistic drone. Whatever it was, this blind man's histrionics must have grated on people's nerves.

So there he is, screaming for Jesus, and all around him are angry people frowning and scolding the noisy guy, and everyone's pushing and maneuvering in the press of the crowd and—suddenly a crazy thing happens.

Jesus turns his face in the blind man's direction. No, there's no fire from heaven blazing forth to quell the disturbance. No, there are no curses or reprimands from Christ. The only people he silences are the ones who've been trying to censor the unrestrained blind man. Jesus says simply, "Tell him to come here." And the rest is a miracle for the history books.

This, I think, is a living picture of what Paul meant when he wrote in 1 Corinthians 13, "Love is patient, love is kind." He wasn't simply throwing out aspirational prose about love. He was describing something he knew intimately, personally. He was describing *Someone* he knew.

I believe this because today (and yesterday too), I was (figuratively) that blind man screaming for Jesus. I expect that sometime tomorrow I may be him again. In fact, for most of my adult life I have tended to scream—in one way or another, sometimes with words, sometimes in actions, sometimes only with tears—*Jesus! Son of David! Have mercy on me!* And this is what I've discovered firsthand, through personal experience:

Jesus always stops. He always listens. He always welcomes me to him, always waits through my tantrums and silences, always points me, somehow, to the way that he will meet my need—even if he must refuse the central desire of my prayer.

Jesus is always patient with me, just as he was with Bartimaeus. Christ is always kind to me, just as he is to you

43

today. And this is what we miss sometimes when we seek answers to the question, "How does Jesus love me?" Yes, we all know what he did for us back on the day he was crucified; what we often forget is what he does for us now, a few thousand years later.

He is patient. Every day, in every moment, when we are frayed and demanding and self-absorbed like children who only want candy and never want a bath. And perhaps because he is patient, *he is kind.* In our harshest moments, when we blame him for pain, when we can't—or won't—admit we need him more than our anger, still, he is kind.

This patient-kind affection is how Jesus is loving you and me right in this exact moment, while I'm writing this sentence and while you read it. I wonder, sometimes, what would happen if we understood how great a difference that kind of love truly makes as it flows through the hidden spaces of our lives.

CLOSET THEOLOGY

[Love] does not envy, it does not boast, it is not proud.

— 1 CORINTHIANS 13:4 (NIV)

Open the door to your closet right now.

Yes, you'll have to take this book along with you, but it's OK. As long as there are no wild animals in there (leopard prints don't count), you should be safe. Spend a moment taking stock of your wardrobe. Go ahead and swish the hangers a bit and puzzle through the shoes. As you do this try to simultaneously take stock of your emotions— what feelings lurk inside you as you stare at the outward expressions of your inward self?

Draw a few emoji that reflect your feelings here.

Look at the emoji you drew. Chances are good that they can all be sorted into one or both of the following categories:

1. Envy. *I wish had more shoes! This dress is so old; I want buy a new one. How is it that I only have three wearable pairs of pants? Oh no, I'm going to have to wear the same shirt twice this week!* Envy always deals with the feeling that you have, or are, somewhat less than what others have (or are). If the clothes in your closet never seem like enough—or perhaps, not good enough—the feeling that twinges inside you is some shade of envy.

2. Pride. *Look at that beautiful suit—I look great in that suit. The only thing missing in this closet is more closet space! 1-2-3 . . . ha! I could wear a different pair of shoes every day for a month. Last time I wore that top I got four compliments at work.* Pride always deals with a certain amount of satisfaction that you or your possessions are somehow better than others. If the clothes in your closet make you swell with satisfaction of quantity or craftsmanship, that feeling you hide inside yourself is some color of pride.

Now, I didn't make you shuffle through your closet just to insult you for having envy or pride. Let's face it, we all deal with those things in many ways. (By the way, the clothes in my closet seem old and shabby to me, so you can guess where I came out in this little experiment!) No, I just wanted you to experience, mildly, what Jesus' love is NOT.

Jesus' love for you does not envy, it does not boast, it is not proud.

If Jesus' love for you does not envy, does not boast, and is not proud . . . what does that mean for you, for today, and for tomorrow? Write your thoughts in the spaces provided—and go ahead and draw new emoji to express your thoughts as well.

1. Jesus' love for me does not envy—what does that mean?

   My Thoughts:

   My Emoji:

2. Jesus' love for me does not boast—what does that mean?

   My Thoughts:

   My Emoji:

3. Jesus' love for me is not proud—what does that mean?

   My Thoughts:

   My Emoji:

RIGHT WORDS, WRONG MOUTHS

[Love] does not dishonor others, it is not self-seeking,
it is not easily angered, it keeps no record of wrongs.

— 1 CORINTHIANS 13:5 (NIV)

"**W**hy do all the right words come out of the all the wrong mouths?"

That was the note in Amy's journal from her college days. She had a crush on a guy who didn't return her attention. At the same time, a few other guys kept pestering her for dates, saying the romantic sentiments she longed to hear—but none of them were the guy that mattered. Right words, wrong mouths.

This is how I feel when I read Paul's lovely sentiments in 1 Corinthians 13:5. Love, he says rapturously, "does not dishonor others, it is not self-seeking, it is not easily angered, it keeps no record of wrongs." If I didn't know Paul better, I'd be happy just to say *Amen* and leave it at that. But I know a little more of Paul's story. His friend, Luke, sold him out when he chronicled the life of the early church in Acts 15:36–40. So I know that Paul once did this (emphasis mine):

After some time Paul said to Barnabas, "Let's go back and visit each city where we previously preached the word of the Lord, to see how the new believers are doing." Barnabas agreed and wanted to take along John Mark. *But Paul disagreed strongly, since John Mark had deserted them* in Pamphylia and had not continued with them in their work. *Their disagreement was so sharp that they separated.* Barnabas took John Mark with him and sailed for Cyprus. Paul chose Silas, and as he left, the believers entrusted him to the Lord's gracious care.

Looking at this event, I wonder how Paul could write 1 Corinthians 13:5 in good conscience. We don't know all the details of their disagreement, but it looks like Paul *dishonored* John Mark by refusing to travel with him; he *sought only his own interests* instead of the interests of either John Mark or Barnabas; he was so *angered* that he broke off his friendship with Barnabas; and he *kept a record of Mark's wrong* (desertion) to the point that it became a hurtful grudge against the young man. I know this isn't baseball, but let's face it, Paul struck out in four at-bats in this situation. So how could he preach to the Corinthians about love's true qualities when he himself didn't live out those qualities?

Was it a "right words, wrong mouth" situation? Maybe, and maybe not. No preacher is perfect, yet all truth is still true. In fact, if God used only perfect people to speak his truth, then none of us would ever hear from God!

And this, I now see, is another way Jesus loves you and me today.

See, I fall short of heaven's standards every day—yet Jesus *does not dishonor* me by withholding his truth from me. He is *not self-seeking*—instead he seeks my benefit even when my words and actions do nothing to help his reputation. He is *not easily angered* toward me and my hypocrisies—preferring to forgive instead of punish. He *keeps no record of wrongs*—choosing his relationship with me each day over his right to hold a grudge against me. He even allows his "right words" to come out of my "wrong mouth" from time to time! And he did the same for the apostle Paul. The result?

Well, years later Paul wrote a letter that indicated he and John Mark both got over the hurt of Acts 15:36–40. In 2 Timothy 4:11, Paul called for the young man to join him again, "Bring Mark with you when you come," he instructed, "for he will be helpful to me in my ministry." Paul, it seems, eventually learned to experience and share the true kind of love he wrote about in 1 Corinthians 13:5.

Why does God allow his right words to be placed in the wrong mouths? I suppose because he cares enough about both the speaker and the hearer to plant those words into their hearts. In this way his example and soul-changing power can eventually grow those people back toward his truth, back to a love that doesn't dishonor, isn't self-seeking, and . . . right, well, you know the rest.

Now, here's the good part. I believe Jesus has done for you what he also did for Paul, and what he daily does for me.

So take a moment right now to stop.

Think about your own relationship with Jesus.

In what ways have you experienced 1 Corinthians 13:5 from him?

Picture them first in your mind. Then sketch out a few images here to remind you of those times. (Yes, stick figures are fine from a brilliant artist like you!) Let your drawings become a prayer of thanks between you and Jesus today. Amen!

WHY?

> Love does not delight in evil but rejoices with
> the truth.
>
> — 1 CORINTHIANS 13:6 (NIV)

Do you sometimes wonder *why* Jesus loves you?

I mean, of course, we all know that God *does* love us because—insert classic children's melody here!—"the Bible tells me so-o-o" (see also John 3:16 and Romans 5:5). And we know that God's love for us is great—see Romans 8:38–39 for a beautiful reminder of that. But seriously, don't you sometimes feel like King David when he wrote the lyrics of Psalm 8:3–4?

> When I look at the night sky and see the work of
> your fingers—the moon and the stars you set in
> place—what are mere mortals that you should
> think about them, human beings that you should
> care for them?

We certainly don't deserve God's love, and he's not obligated to love either. In fact, some people believe God doesn't actually love us. They think instead that either he doesn't exist or he is/was a Being who created everything and set it all in motion—then decided to disengage and maintain distance from us. To them God (if he exists) is like some kind of cosmic Watcher fascinated by the soap opera events of Planet Earth, but certainly not a personal deity who'd bother to love the ants he created. Obviously I think that perspective is fatally flawed, but still I sometimes wonder . . .

Why does Jesus love you and me?

I'm no expert on what motivates our God, but if you'll grant me a little license to share my opinion, here's what I think:

Love . . . rejoices with the truth.

For me, that offers at least a plausible explanation for the impossible love God relentlessly showers on us. And it's why I think Jesus loves me, and you, and all the other people out there: Because Christ alone knows the full truth about who he is and what he created—the truth about *who* we are, *why* we are, and *what* he is doing in us.

Listen to just a few of the sound bites Scripture has shared with us in that regard:

And because we are his children, God has sent the Spirit of his Son into our hearts, prompting us to call out, "Abba, Father." —GALATIANS 4:6

And I am certain that God, who began the good work within you, will continue his work until it

is finally finished on the day when Christ Jesus
returns. —PHILIPPIANS 1:6

*

For we are God's masterpiece. He has created us
anew in Christ Jesus, so we can do the good things
he planned for us long ago. —EPHESIANS 2:10

*

You are a chosen people. You are royal priests,
a holy nation, God's very own possession.
—1 PETER 2:9

*

.But to all who believed him and accepted him,
he gave the right to become children of God.
—JOHN 1:12

See, Christ's love for you has very little to do with you and
everything to do with him. His love is not simply some cosmic
feeling of kindness, but an eternal truth about *who he is and
who you are to him.* Likewise, God's eternal truth about you
is not simply an emotionless fact, but is an eternal passion
based in who he is and what he's doing with you *as his.*

Put simply, Jesus loves because he alone knows—and
rejoices in—the full truth about himself and what he's doing
in us. He loves us not because he must choose to do so or
because he feels obligated to constantly manufacture an
emotion akin to compassion. He loves us because *that* is the

truth of who he is—our joyful, eternal truth. At least that's my impression.

What do you think?

1. Why does Jesus love you? Explain it as if to a friend.

2. What do you think it means for love to "rejoice with the truth"? How have you seen that in action?

3. What truths do you know about love? Make a list, and then make your list into a prayer.

THE DEBIT CARD TEST

[Love] always protects, always trusts, always hopes, always perseveres.

— 1 CORINTHIANS 13:7

Look at the list below. Next to each item, write the name of someone who fits that description in your life. (Use a different name for each item, and feel free to skip any that don't apply.)

- Rock Star

- Best Friend

- Celebrity

- Sibling

- Coworker

- Spouse

- Parent

- Church Member

- Athlete

- Child

- Neighbor

- Facebook Friend

- TV Preacher

Ready? OK—now open your purse or wallet and take out your debit or credit card. Lay it down next to this book. Look at your card, then look at the names on your list. Do this a few times.

Now imagine that, one by one, each person on your list has come up to you and asked:

"Would you loan me your card for a week or so?"

Is there anyone on your list to whom you'd say, "Sure, I'll give my card to you right now!"? What emotion do you feel about loaning your card to that person? Write it next to his or her name.

Are there others to whom you'd refuse to loan your debit card? What emotions come to mind when you think of loaning your card to them? Write those emotions next to the appropriate people above.

OK, you can put your card away. Look at your list again. I'm sure there are lots of psychological nuances embedded in the decisions you made and the emotions you listed—but we'll let therapy take care of that! What I want you to notice is this:

If there's at least one person on the list above to whom you'd loan your debit or credit card without reservation, chances are very good it's a person you know and *love*— and a person you believe loves you. The reason for that is because *you are a vulnerable person* (in ways too numerous to tally up here), and your vulnerability feels heightened when your financial resources are at risk. So you instinctively trust in love, which then allows you to trust the object of your love with your money.

This little exercise is designed simply to remind you (safely) of that feeling of vulnerability you hide from others—and even from yourself at times—and how that angsty sense of impending doom is comforted by a relationship defined by love. Will you loan your debit card to your best friend of the last 20 years? Sure. How about to that TV preacher who suddenly shows up at your front door and begs for a generous donation? Um, no.

The Person to whom you are most vulnerable—the One to whom you are laid bare in body, soul, and spirit—is Jesus himself. Were he fallible like you or me, this level of vulnerability would be concerning.

Thankfully, he is neither you nor me, and his love is so reliable that our weakness becomes both safety and strength in him. We can entrust ourselves, all our frailties, to Christ because *we know the way his love responds to our vulnerabilities*:

Jesus always protects.

When we're careless about our spiritual health, when we're prideful toward him and others, when we unfairly blame him for our pain, he takes the harshest penalties on himself instead of placing them on us.

Jesus always trusts.

When we wander away from his guidance, when we call his truth a lie, when we break faith with him, still he refuses to be unfaithful toward us.

Jesus always hopes.

When we feel like giving up, when we distrust his promises, when we fail and fail again, he refuses to give up on us or to cancel his plans for us.

Jesus always perseveres.

When we stumble into habitual sin, when we act like hypocrites, when we sever relationships he meant us to keep intact, still he remains with us, always at work to bring out his beauty in our lives, no matter if it takes him an eternity.

This is how Jesus loves you today—right now—so that even in your most vulnerable moments, you can find rest and confidence in the safety of his love.

Remember that next time you pull out your debit card at the grocery store, OK?

TATTOO OPTIONAL

Love never fails.

— 1 CORINTHIANS 13:8 (NIV)

Today is about prompting your eyes to see what heaven already knows, about helping your mind understand what your heart sometimes has trouble believing:

Jesus' love for you never fails.

My first thought was to suggest that you go out and get a tattoo of the phrase "Love never fails" from 1 Corinthians 13:8. You'd always remember it then, wouldn't you? But have no fear, cooler heads have prevailed. We'll make this a "tattoo optional" day and focus instead on our real goal. Here's how we'll do it.

1. First, you'll need a big sticky note and a pen or marker.

2. On the sticky note, write in large print: "LOVE NEVER FAILS."

3. Place your sticky note firmly on the cover of this book—and you're ready!

Now, for the rest of today, I'm asking you to carry this book—with your note on it—everywhere you go. And I mean everywhere! To work, in meetings, at lunch, at the coffeehouse with your friends, at your daughter's volleyball game, in the doctor's office, in the crook of your arm when you go for a walk or run on the treadmill, next to your plate as you eat dinner, in your lap while you watch TV, all the way to your bedside before you go to sleep tonight. Anyplace you go, bring this book—with the sticky note—along with you. Don't hide it in your purse or backpack, don't leave it in your car or pushed into a corner on your kitchen counter. Keep the book, and your note, front and center all day long. Yes, people will ask you about it, and yes you'll probably have to tell a friend or two (and maybe a stranger) what you're doing. That's OK. In fact, that's a good thing.

See, today, *all of the day*, I want you to make your prayer to God the same as King David's prayer of old:

Let me hear of your unfailing love each morning, for I am trusting you. Show me where to walk, for I give myself to you. —PSALM 143:8

The goal today is for your sticky note and this book to remind you constantly to look, and listen, and pay attention to the unique ways God demonstrates his unfailing love toward you each day. Maybe it will even spark a conversation or two—who knows?

Our human default pattern is simply to take his reliable goodness for granted, to miss the expressions of persistent love Christ lavishes on us each morning. But not today, and not you, right?

So, pick up this book and lay it down again in places where you'll see it no matter where you are or what you do. And with your own handwriting as your reminder, set your senses on high alert to recognize and identify any expression of Christ's enduring love for you. What does that look like? You can decide—maybe you'll be surprised too. Every time you spot evidence of his love in your life today, open up this book and write it down in the space provided here.

Let your cumulative notes become the substance of your prayer to Jesus before you nod off to sleep tonight.

Have fun!

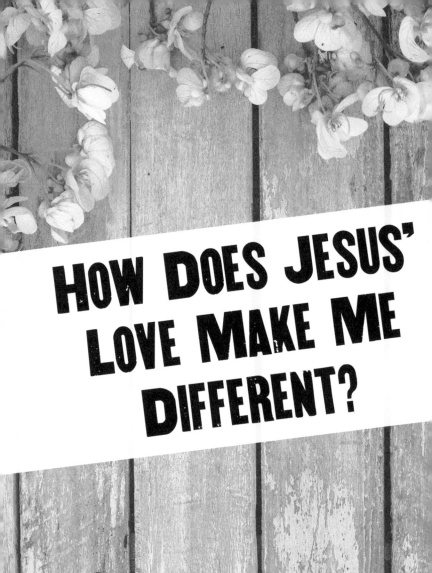

HOW DOES JESUS' LOVE MAKE ME DIFFERENT?

JESUS . . . ALWAYS

To illustrate the point further, Jesus told them this story: "A man had two sons. The younger son told his father, 'I want my share of your estate now before you die.' So his father agreed to divide his wealth between his sons.

"A few days later this younger son packed all his belongings and moved to a distant land, and there he wasted all his money in wild living. About the time his money ran out, a great famine swept over the land, and he began to starve. He persuaded a local farmer to hire him, and the man sent him into his fields to feed the pigs. The young man became so hungry that even the pods he was feeding the pigs looked good to him. But no one gave him anything.

"When he finally came to his senses, he said to himself, 'At home even the hired servants have food enough to spare, and here I am dying of hunger! I will go home to my father and say, "Father, I have sinned against both heaven and you, and I am no longer worthy of being called your son. Please take me on as a hired servant."'

"So he returned home to his father. And while he was still a long way off, his father saw him coming. Filled with love and compassion, he ran to his son, embraced him, and kissed him. His son said to him, 'Father, I have sinned against both heaven and you, and I am no longer worthy of being called your son.'

"But his father said to the servants, 'Quick! Bring the finest robe in the house and put it on him. Get a ring for his finger and sandals for his feet. And kill the calf we have been fattening. We must celebrate with a feast, for this son of mine was dead and has now returned to life. He was lost, but now he is found.' So the party began.

"Meanwhile, the older son was in the fields working. When he returned home, he heard music and dancing in the house, and he asked one of the servants what was going on. 'Your brother is back,' he was told, 'and your father has killed the fattened calf. We are celebrating because of his safe return.'

"The older brother was angry and wouldn't go in. His father came out and begged him, but he replied, 'All these years I've slaved for you and never once refused to do a single thing you told me to. And in all that time you never gave me even one young goat for a feast with my friends. Yet when this son of yours comes back after squandering your money on prostitutes, you celebrate by killing the fattened calf!'

"His father said to him, 'Look, dear son, you have always stayed by me, and everything I have is yours. We had to celebrate this happy day. For your brother was dead and has come back to life! He was lost, but now he is found!'"

—LUKE 15:11–32

Use this page to journal your thoughts and prayers about what you've read today. Feel free to use the questions below as prompts, or to write whatever else is on your mind.

1. What does Luke 15:11–32 say to you about Jesus' "love and compassion" for you?

2. Why do you suppose Jesus wanted you to know this parable?

3. What do you think happened to the prodigal son *after* the party—the next day, the next month, the next year, the rest of his life? Tell that story here.

THOUGHTS OF HOME

"I will go home to my father . . ."

— LUKE 15:18

Have you ever seen a burning bridge?

I watched one once on the news from Atlanta, a fire that closed the I-85 freeway and made a huge section of the road collapse onto the ground below.[2] Massive plumes of dark smoke filled the air, traffic backed up for miles, tons of steel-reinforced, blackened concrete crumbled like a child's Play-Doh creation. Even after the best efforts of firefighters and safety personnel, the blaze still smoldered for hours afterward.

A fire like that never really burns out, does it? Given some months of strenuous effort and work, that bridge on I-85 can be rebuilt, possibly made even stronger than before. But once you've seen something like that go up in flames right before your eyes, watched it be reduced to scorched earth and impassable terrain, how do you eject that image permanently from your mind? You can't. It remains with you always.

Unlike the burning of I-85, a bridge burned in ancient times was usually an act of war. Roman armies were known to cross into enemy territory, then burn the bridge behind them in a "conquer or die" display.[3] The spectacle of that burned bridge was meant to strike fear into enemies—and inspire desperation for victory within Roman warriors. Retreat was no longer an option. That burning bridge was a statement of finality to every soldier:

You can never go back. You can never go home.

Looking at Luke 15:11–32, I see something akin to what the ancient Romans legionnaires saw, something like the fiery obstacle those I-85 freeway drivers encountered on their way home:

A bridge up in flames.

"I want my share of your estate now before you die," the younger son says to the father (15:12), and the first torch is lit. In that time, like today, a child's inheritance wasn't given until the father had passed away. To demand it of your *living* dad was an insult tantamount to saying, "I wish you were dead already, because I love your things more than I love you."[4] But that wasn't all.

"A few days later this younger son packed all his belongings and moved to a distant land" (15:13). Now the bridge between father and son is engulfed in flames. The road that should've led to family, to father—to *home*—is destroyed. When this callous kid cashed out his inheritance, insulted his father and older brother, and chose to embrace life as a voluntary exile in a pagan land, he declared himself as good as dead to all he had known, to all the people who had once loved him.

Bridges burned. Conquer or die. No turning back.

Right?

Well, that's the way it should've been. But today I read the boy's thoughts when he'd lost everything, when he suffered under the punishment of his own foolish actions, and I heard him say: "I will go *home* to my father . . ." (Luke 15:18, emphasis mine).

Wait . . . what?

The place where his father lives is no more his home than the pigsty where he longs to eat disgusting pods meant for swine. He has no more right to call his father's house "home" than you or I have to call the White House our vacation rental property. After all he's done, after all the people he's hurt, what makes the Prodigal dare to believe that he still has a "home" anywhere in the world?

I suppose it's because, no matter where he lives, no matter what he does, no matter how much of his father's possessions he sells, or abuses, or discards, one thing always remains true:

He is his father's son.

There's nothing he can do, say, or think that can ever change that fact. It's who he is whether he wants it to be true or not. And so, as long as the father has a home, the son always has someplace to go—one place in the world that he can always call "home"—even from far away, even when lost and starving as a consequence of his own sin.

And where there is home, there is hope.

I will go home to my father . . .

A true home is a place that heals, that nourishes. It's where we dream of our tomorrows, and find little joys in today. It's the place where we feel safe from the outside world, where we sigh and let our bellies hang out after holding them in all day. A true home is that one place we must have, where we can feel, however briefly, like maybe, just maybe, everything is going to be OK.

Now, with that image of home in mind, let's take a second look at that burning bridge we discussed earlier, thinking about what the Prodigal always having a home means for us.

When we turn our backs on God and his ways, his truth . . .

When we run away and hide, disregarding his hope and faithfulness in our lives . . .

When we cry out to money, or position, or power as our means of salvation from petty problems . . .

When we puff out our chests and fall on our faces . . .

When our dreams are dashed, and the consequences of our sinful actions have left us alone and helpless in a hurtful world . . .

Christ always welcomes us *home.*

We burn our bridges, yet God refuses to let them crumble like scorched concrete. We light the torch and set our circumstances ablaze, yet Jesus refuses to let our reckless firestorms burn up the path back to him.

Instead, God always invites us back to the place where he is our safety and our provision, to come home to our Father.

Yes, sometimes we still have to suffer the consequences of our actions. No, we never have to suffer alone. Yes, the home Jesus offers to us is spiritual and not physical (yet), and this is sometimes hard. But it doesn't have to discourage us, because our real home is not "where the heart is," but *where Jesus is*. And no fiery inferno can ever take that spiritual home from us.

So we ask, how does Jesus' love make me different? My first answer—and I hope yours—is the same as that Prodigal who tried so hard to burn every bridge between him and his father:

Because of Christ's love for me, I can always,
always,
always say:
I will go home.

WELCOME (ALWAYS HAPPY TO SEE YOU)

Filled with love and compassion, he ran to his son, embraced him, and kissed him.

— LUKE 15:20

Where are you always welcome? Or to be more specific, where could you go, right now, today, and know with absolute certainty that you belonged there and the people would be happy to see you?

Sketch out a representation of the door to that place here.

What do you feel when you think about this place? Write your feelings out as words that decorate your door.

It feels good to think of this place, no? It feels like *home*, I suspect, to picture the faces of loved ones, family or friends or coworkers, or even just familiar furniture that brings comfort and seems to have been made just for you. Take a breath now and hold it long enough to revel in the memory of your happy place, of this "home" represented by your door.

Good. Well done.

Now, may I tell you a hard truth?

For too many of us—maybe you?—this little imagination exercise is impossible to complete. Today when I did this devotion there were at least two or three "doors" I could draw ... but I've had times in my life when no door, no place in this big, wide world felt like it would open happily to me with joy waiting on the other side.

Some months after my wife died from cancer, a friend asked me, "What do you miss most about Amy?"

I barely had to think about it.

"She smiled whenever I walked into the room," I said. "For 30 years, every time she saw me, she smiled."

You might be surprised by how much strength that gives to a person, how much hope, to always be welcomed. No, not just welcomed. To always be *wanted*. Because of Amy, any door could open into a happy place for me—all I needed was for her to be on the other side of it. And even as she was dying, when she slept for twenty hours a day and was awake only minutes at time, if Amy opened her eyes and saw

74

me sitting near her hospice bed, she smiled. Sometimes she wouldn't even say a word, she'd just smile at me, then close her eyes again and drift back to sleep . . . until the awful day came when her eyes no longer opened and that smile no longer appeared. And suddenly I couldn't think of a single place where I belonged, of a single "home" where I'd always be welcomed.

Death has not been the only closed door in my life, and I'm sure that's been your experience too. And when you've lost the person or place that feels like home, where can you go to feel welcomed again?

Look at the drawing of your door above.

Now take your pen or marker and—no matter how beautiful you think that door is—draw an enormous, ugly "X" right through the middle of it. Scribble through your drawing until it's clear that this door does not belong to you anymore.

How would you feel if you knew you could never go through that door again?

The feeling that twinges inside you now is just a fraction of the grief our Prodigal must have felt, lost in a land far from his home. Penniless, sickly, humiliated, forgotten. No place where he felt welcomed. No place to belong. No place to call ho—

Wait a minute.

Do you see that? (Go ahead and squint if it helps you.)

Here is our boy, walking down the dusty road, dirty and unwanted. Tired, a failure, and hoping just to get a low-paying job from the man he used to call Father. His feet are callused and sore. Is he limping? His stomach is clenched, and his temples are beginning to throb. Still he takes each step forward.

He is not welcome here, he knows that. But he came anyway. And now . . .

His eyes catch movement in the distance. His gaze lifts from the ground and his cracked lips fall slightly apart.

Filled with love and compassion, the lost boy's father is *running* to his son, welcoming him home with arms wide open, with joy spilling out in a broad, spectacular smile.

The Prodigal has finally returned to the one person who makes this place somewhere he belongs.

Freeze that picture in your mind right now. Memorize it, because in that scene we can see most clearly another powerful way that Jesus' love makes us different—how his love makes us strong, gives us hope.

When we come to our heavenly Father, in sorrow or in joy, in anger or repentance, in sickness or in strength—however we come to him!—God is always happy to see us.

And chances are good that he's smiling.

WHAT IS GOD THINKING??

"Father, I have sinned against both heaven and you . . ."

— LUKE 15:21

I wonder why God sometimes gives us what we ask for—all the while knowing that what we ask for just might kill us. Or harm others. Or hurt his reputation. Or tempt us into being prideful, awful people. Or drive away those who might have turned to him if not for our poor examples of so-called faith. Or . . . well, you get the idea.

This is the question I'm wrestling with today, as I read afresh Jesus' parable of the prodigal son in Luke 15. I know that, in this story, our heavenly Father is represented by the ungrateful boy's dad. And I know that the ungrateful son, well, he might as well be played by me, or by you, because in the Prodigal we easily see ourselves and our sinful attitudes toward God, our loving Father.

When I read the boy's candid assessment of his life in Luke 15:21, it makes me feel like weeping. "I have sinned . . ."

Can you imagine if the sum total of your life amounted to that? If they asked you to title your own biopic ("now playing in theatres everywhere!"), and the best, most honest name you could give your movie was, "I Have Sinned"?

Maybe you've read about, or even remember, the televangelist Jim Bakker from his popular TV show of the 1970s and '80s, *Praise the Lord*. His famous abuses of power, money-hungry approach to ministry, and sexual misconduct are the stuff of legend—except they really happened. What I remember most about this man is that after his rise, and fall, and jail time, and divorce, he finally wrote a book telling his life story. When it was time to attach a title to the book, the best, most honest name he could give to describe his entire past was: *I Was Wrong*.

When I first saw a copy of that book, I remember thinking, *How tragic to have that be the epitaph for a life. Why didn't God stop him before he could do all that damage?*

And when I read the Prodigal's similar statement, "Father, I have sinned against both heaven and you," I have the same thought, and I wonder:

Why didn't the father simply say "no"?

See, it was well within the father's power to deny that ungrateful son his evil desire. When the boy hatefully demanded his inheritance *now*, there's not a single one of us who would've faulted ol' dad for saying, "Nope. Now go back to the field and get to work."

Consider just a few of the predictable consequences of the boy's demands:

- The father's family was divided.

- The value of the father's carefully built estate was diminished by 1/3—a lifetime of work erased in one day.

- After being lavished with a fortune in cash from the father's hand, the boy simply wasted it all. In fact, that's why we call him "prodigal," because that term literally means *wasteful*.[5]

- Israel—and the reputation of Israel's most holy God—was mocked and insulted in the eyes of unbelievers (pagans) by the son's flamboyantly unrighteous example in their midst.

- The father's beloved son was physically imperiled, socially and emotionally humiliated, and forced to submit to work in a religiously unclean pigsty.

- The father endured years of grief over his beloved son who was now lost and presumed dead.

Knowing that these awful outcomes would be only some of the consequences of granting the son's demand, why would the father ever say yes? Likewise, since God knows the horrible outcomes of every one of our self-absorbed prayers . . . why does he sometimes allow them to be fulfilled?

I can't know the answer with certainty, but I think it has something to do with *the way his love acts to makes us different*.

If I were "God," my first impulse would be to build fences and lock doors and dispatch angels and make sure my kids could never do anything to bring harm to themselves. Not on my watch, right? But . . . if I'm that kind of father, then what kind of child have I just described?

A baby.

A tiny, helpless, ignorant, incontinent, slobbery tot.

And if I were to let that baby stay within that extreme parental protection, well, let's just say I'd still be changing diapers when my boy hits retirement age! It reminds me of Paul's reprimand to the Christians in Corinth:

> Dear brothers and sisters, when I was with you I couldn't talk to you as I would to spiritual people. I had to talk . . . as though you were infants in Christ. I had to feed you with milk, not with solid food, because you weren't ready for anything stronger.
> —1 CORINTHIANS 3:1–2

While I honestly hate the inevitable harm that comes when God allows me to make sinful, selfish decisions, I can also see (at least dimly) that he's got more in mind that just my immediate consequences. Same goes for you too. Our Father loves us enough to let suffering shape us, mature and grow us, *change* us into women and men who begin to understand—and live out—what his heart and intentions for us really are. Our Father is even willing to grieve for now, knowing he (and we!) will be able to rejoice one day when we finally leave childish things behind (see 1 Corinthians 13:11).

I see this now in the father in Christ's parable as well. He's a dad who will allow—even enable—his son to discover for himself that life apart from the father is a wasted existence that ends with an epitaph reading, "I have sinned."

It's a difficult truth, but a good and holy one as well. Jesus loves us enough to sometimes let us learn for ourselves—the hard way, through experience and pain—how his patient love can change us, make us into

different . . .

better . . .

humbler . . .

more generous people . . .

Like him.

All right, that was a lot to digest today! So take time to think about it, then journal your thoughts and prayers about what you read. Feel free to follow one or both of the prompts below, or to write whatever else is on your mind.

1. What questions do you have after reading today's devotion? What will you do to arrive at possible answers to those questions?

2. How will you title the book (or movie) of your life? Why? (Go ahead and sketch the movie poster if you feel like it!)

A PARTY IS REQUIRED

"We must celebrate with a feast, for this son of mine was dead and has now returned to life. He was lost, but now he is found." So the party began.

— LUKE 15:23–24

I must admit I'm fascinated by the life of Dion Rich.

Haven't heard of him? Well, if you search the internet chances are good you'll find a photo of him hoisting Tom Landry, legendary coach of the Dallas Cowboys, on his shoulders for a victory ride after the 'Boys' championship at Super Bowl XII. Or you might find him sitting next to actress Nicole Kidman at the Academy Awards ceremony. Or arm-in-arm with Washington Redskins coach Joe Gibbs at yet another Super Bowl. Or standing beside the track at the Kentucky Derby or even the Olympic Games.

No, he's not a celebrity, nor is he a coach, the owner of a race horse, or an Olympic athlete. Dion Rich is, it might be said, the world's greatest gate crasher. In fact, he got so good at sneaking into parties that he successfully crashed 33 (count 'em, 33!) Super Bowl games.

Sports Illustrated writer Rick Reilly followed him into Super Bowl XXXVI. It was held just a few months after 9/11, on February 3, 2002. Security for "the Big Dance" cost the NFL millions of dollars, and included Secret Service agents, FBI, FEMA, National Guard, and US Marshals. Pretending to be a referee wasn't going to cut it. Working his charms in a wheelchair wouldn't do either. Something from his bag of fake press credentials? Nope, not in this well-guarded castle.

So what happened? According to Reilly, "The fortress lost. Rich was inside in six minutes. I followed him the whole way. It was pure art."

At the first security station, Dion Rich managed to catch a guard with her head buried in someone else's bag and, quick as lightning, squeezed unnoticed past her and through a one-foot gap between a metal detector and a fence. Next he slid around a guy distracted by his duties of scanning people with a metal detector wand, faded into the crowd to get past a National Guardsman—all this simply to get up to the place where the ticket-takers stood in place.

But the ticket-takers were no match for Dion. He found a row of doors that locked from the inside and simply waited. Sure enough, it wasn't long before a hurried supervisor came barreling out of one of the doors. Before it could close, Rich was there—literally—with his foot in the door. In a flash, he was inside for the big game.

Reilly reports, "I didn't hear from Dion again until midnight. He called from inside the [St. Louis] Rams postgame party. . . . Thank God he's on our side."[6]

Without endorsing his obviously illegal activities, let me say that Dion Rich shows more courage in his gate-crashing endeavors than most of us do in our spiritual lives as children of our heavenly Father. Dion Rich figures he *belongs* at the party—whether he's invited or not!

How about you?

In Jesus' parable of the prodigal, we see the father (who represents God) pulling out all the stops to create a grand celebration simply because his lost son has been found. In fact, I'm struck by his exact words in that regard: "We *must* celebrate..."

Yet outside the party stands the older son, refusing to go in, angry and jealous, assuming the party is for someone else—despite the father's impassioned entreaties for him to join in the joy (Luke 15:28).

I have a good friend, let's call him Rex. He tells me that for most of his adult life, spiritually speaking, he felt similarly uninvited to God's party. He described it to me this way: Rex saw himself standing outside in the cold, looking through a window. Inside a feast was going on, with happy revelers warmed by the glow. Jesus sat at the head of the party and when he looked up and saw Rex standing outside ... all he would do was frown and shake his head. In Rex's eyes, Christ's big celebration was not for him.

My poor friend suffered this awful misconception until well into his fifties when he finally, FINALLY, realized:

God's party is for him (and me, and you). Rex doesn't have to suffer outside that joy, or even make like Dion Rich and try to find a way to break in. The door is open, arms are spread wide! Rex *belongs* at that fantastic spiritual gathering.

How about you? Are you still trying to gate-crash your way into God's love and joy? Give up the struggle, friend, and take your rightful place at your heavenly Father's side. You see, when God looks at you, coming to him for comfort and relief like that helpless Prodigal Son, he is very happy to have you near. Your Father understands that your return to him each day means *a party is required*. And you're not just invited—you're the reason for God's generous, unbridled joy.

Take that, gate-crasher.

Use this space to journal your thoughts and prayers about what you read. Feel free to follow one or both of the prompts below, or write whatever else is on your mind.

1. When do you feel like you don't belong at "God's party"? Explain.

2. When the Prodigal returned, the father insisted, "We must celebrate . . ." How can you join that spiritual celebration today, right here, right now?

JUDGING THE DISTANCE

The older brother was angry and wouldn't go in.
His father came out and begged him . . .

— LUKE 15:28

From where you're sitting, look up and gauge the distance between you and the closest door. Don't use standard feet or inches as your measurement guide: instead, use the spine of this book.

Take another look at the door, and at this book. If you were to lay *29 Days to Different* down on the floor, and flip it lengthwise time and again, how many "book spines" would it take for you to reach the door?

Write your guess here:

All right, go ahead and measure the distance between you and the closest door in book spines, then come back here and note how close you were to the right number. Ready, go!

Write the real book-spine distance here:

How do you feel about your guess?

Were you close?

Did you (gasp!) get it EXACTLY right?

You can play this game with anything—bottle caps, pencils, LEGO® blocks and action figures, whatever. It's fun, but what if there were something riding on your guess? What if there were consequences for getting it wrong?

What if the measurement you made in book spines was going to be used by a blind man walking to the edge of the Grand Canyon? How would you feel about your guess then? Sure, you might be close, maybe only two-thirds of a book-spine from perfect. But if a blind man trusted you enough to follow your judgment, close wouldn't be good enough.

Or look at it another way. What if you had to jump across the canyon? And what if, despite your super-powered leap, you came down with the opposite side of the canyon still two-thirds of a book spine away from your farthest reach? Misjudgment is harmless when the stakes are low, but when there are consequences, well, that's a different emotion, isn't it?

I once had a friend tell me I was a terrorist threat and so would not be allowed in a certain building ever again. Reality be damned. He'd heard it from some third party and decided to believe it without even talking to me. (I am an

Arab-American, right? So why not a terrorist?) He wouldn't even allow me to respond to the false accusation. What could I do? I left and never went back. But that gross misjudgment of my character still makes knots roll up in my stomach. *How could my friend ever believe such a spectacularly hateful lie about me?*

I'm guessing you've never been called a terrorist, but probably you've felt something of what I felt in that moment. Do you remember that time when someone— maybe your friends, maybe your family—grossly misjudged you? And do you remember how you felt? Describe those feelings here:

Here's why we're exploring the emotions that accompany misjudgment: I think that sometimes, maybe often, we misjudge the character and intent of our heavenly Father. That's what the older son did, right? He came back from working in the field and found a party going on. Instead of joining the celebration, he misjudged his father's affection and intent, and so "The older brother was angry and wouldn't go in."

It's very easy to judge God's actions only in the context of our happiness and immediate desires. The problem is, when we misjudge God in those ways and get upset about what we think he is or is not doing in our lives, those hateful emotions rebound inward and take up residence in us until they grow into bitterness, selfishness, or even hurtfulness of ourselves and others. Those feelings separate us from the family that God intends us to be as his children. Let me show you what I mean.

When my good friend Kent (of the apple tree parable) tells stories of growing up, I sometimes want to cringe. If the boy stubbed his toe or scraped his knee, a well-meaning grandmother was quick to pounce—and pronounce, "Jesus is punishing you!" To her, it was simple: You sin. God smites you. That gross misjudgment of God planted deep, distrustful roots in Kent's soul. For him, God was always antagonistic, always watching and frowning, constantly ready to unleash war against his misbehaving kids. It took decades—and seminary and a lifetime in church leadership—before Kent was finally able to come into God's presence without secret fear, before he could believe for himself the truth he'd read and preached: "We have peace with God because of what Jesus Christ our Lord has done for us" (Romans 5:1).

My old pastor, Chuck Swindoll, says it this way, "No circumstance is the result of [God's] punishment. Bad things do not happen because we have been bad. No event is an expression of God's ill will against us. On the contrary, He has promised to use every circumstance . . . to guide His own to maturity."[7]

I wonder how long it will take us to actually believe that?

All right, enough preaching. Take a last look at the distance between you and the closest door. Maybe you misjudged that distance in book-spine lengths. Honestly? No big deal.

Now imagine yourself "seeing" into the spiritual realm. How do you judge the distance between you and God?

PRACTICE FOR HEAVEN

So the party began.

— LUKE 15:24

Here's what we know: Your heavenly Father is happy to see you.

In fact, because of his unfailing love for you, the simple fact that you choose to be near to him (in the spiritual sense for now) is cause for celebration in heaven. Honestly, I'm not sure what that looks like, but I do know that knowledge changes me—and you. Christ loves us enough to initiate celebrations with us. That's a whole new perspective, isn't it?

So, let's do this today: Plan a party!

We'll call it "practice for heaven," for the moment when eternity becomes reality, when Jesus' love is something we can actually touch and embrace.

Now, what do you want to do?

If it's spring or summer, you might plan a cookout with burgers and brats and all the fixins. Maybe invite your friends and neighbors to join you, and when they ask what the reason is for your celebration, just smile and say, "I'm practicing for heaven."

If it's fall or winter, make it an indoor fest, with hot chocolate and roasted marshmallows and possibly even a song or two.

Or maybe you plan an intimate dinner party with a few close friends or your spouse—a celebration of how Jesus' love empowers you to love each other. Or a family "Jesus Loves Us!" party with backyard games and, of course, ice cream.

Want to dream even bigger?

What if you (and a few of your generous friends) rent a hall and hire a DJ and throw a "It's Not a Wedding, but Come Have Fun Anyway!" bash for a few hundred people? Maybe invite everyone at your church—and tell them to bring friends and neighbors as well. Yeah, this one would cost a few thousand dollars, so don't try to do it alone. And maybe it's too big even for a group, but you can still have fun planning the event.

Regardless of what you plan, this is your chance to tell yourself again, "Wow, Jesus loves ME. It's time to celebrate that fact!"

Write your plans in the space provided. Feel free to plan two or three variations, if you like. Then pick a date—sometime in the next three months or so, if possible—and make at least one of your ideas happen. After all, God has not only given you permission, he's set an example for you, with an invitation to join in:

So the party began . . .

PARTY THEME

VENUE

GUEST LIST

FOOD IDEAS

ENTERTAINMENT IDEAS

NOW WHAT?

JESUS . . . IN ME

We love because he first loved us.

— 1 JOHN 4:19 (NIV)

Use this space to journal your thoughts and prayers about what you've read today. Feel free to follow one or both of the prompts below, or to write whatever else is on your mind.

1. Play the "If . . . Then . . ." game with 1 John 4:19. Ask yourself, "IF this Scripture is true for me today, THEN what does that mean for me tomorrow?"

2. Now play the "If . . . Why . . ." game. Looking again at 1 John 4:19, ask yourself, "IF this Scripture is true, WHY do I have trouble living it in my daily experience?"

ALL OF THE CHRISTIAN LIFE

We love because he first loved us.

— 1 JOHN 4:19 (NIV)

All of the Christian life is an expression of gratitude.

Whenever I say this for the first time to a friend, the typical response is, "Um, what?" followed by a gentle pat on my shoulder along with an expression of, "Poor Mike. The old guy's finally lost it." There are a few exceptions, sure, but most stare at me for a moment and then tell me the same thing my buddy Eric said after thinking it over for about two weeks, "That can't be right, Mike. It's too easy."

Sigh.

I get it. We've been raised in Sunday school and church services and told we're sinners in the hands of an angry God. We know that Scripture places prime importance on good behavior and right living and doing good works, and our teachers and preachers tell us constantly to "live as if you're the only Jesus someone will see!" It makes sense, and the intent is usually good, but that outside-in approach is a backward way to live a life of faith.

A lot of people really struggle with this concept, but once you get it, it's an unbelievable, freeing truth:

All of the truly good and holy things that you think and do in your Christian life are your living expressions of gratitude for what Christ has done for you.

If your good and holy behaviors are mostly obligations you try to live up to, a list of "ought tos" and "have tos," then you've missed the truth—and joy!—of authentic Christian living and spiritual growth.

Once Jesus' enemies tried to trap and discredit him with deceitful theological questions about religious belief and practice.

One of them, an expert in the law, tested him with this question: "Teacher, which is the greatest commandment in the Law [of Moses]?"

Jesus replied: "'Love the Lord your God with all your heart and with all your soul and with all your mind.' This is the first and greatest commandment. And the second is like it: 'Love your neighbor as yourself.' *All the Law and the Prophets hang on these two commandments.*"

—MATTHEW 22:35–40 NIV (emphasis mine)

Huh.

ALL of Moses' law and the Old Testament prophetic teachings hang on something as simple as love? Every last bit of it?

If that's true, then the question becomes not only "how can we love?" but also "why can we love?" The answer to both questions is as fresh today as it was when the apostle John explained it thousands of years ago: *We love because he first loved us.*

Gratitude grows authentically out of the experience of being loved, which in turn empowers us to love from the inside out. That's where our authentic good works begin, from deep within our hearts (see Psalm 9:1, Proverbs 4:23, Matthew 15:18, among others). When that happens, living a faith-filled life is no longer a burden of expectation and failure. Instead, love becomes a natural, normal thing. There's work, sure, but not toil, because holy work done gratefully produces its own joy, an authenticity of Spirit that empowers and energizes us.

Sadly, though, too many of us keep trying to change ourselves (and others) from the outside in (see Matthew 23:27–28), and are always surprised when we fail.

I visited a church not long ago. It was a large one—a bona fide megachurch. At the appropriate time, the pastor encouraged us all to "greet one another in Jesus' love." You know what happens next, right? You shake a few hands, mumble a few "good mornings" and take your seat sixty seconds later none the worse for wear, even if none the wiser. I was near the back, and there weren't many folks in that area, so I shook a hand to my right, saw no one else nearby, and started to sit back down.

Bam!

A fist hit me in the shoulder. I turned to my left and found a man standing behind me, grimacing, palm outstretched for a handshake. I hadn't seen him, so he hit me.

I shook his hand. His fingers barely touched mine, then he broke off, snorted at me in disgust, and rolled his eyes as he returned to his seat.

I don't know what his story is or what was going on with him that day, but although he technically greeted me with an expression of love that Sunday morning, there was nothing genuinely loving about the encounter.

I'm afraid this surface-level, obligatory expression of love describes much of the Christian life for many of us. We're so obsessed with *acting* love, we forget the gratifying truth of *why* we love. We take for granted the enormity of what we've been given, so instead of letting genuine gratitude govern our hearts and prompt our actions, we substitute acceptable outward expressions for inward transformation. We're so much poorer for it, yet we continue to perversely think this legalistic poverty makes us rich. It's tragic.

Do you know *why* you can love, *why* God's Spirit in you can help you fulfill the greatest commandments that Jesus spoke of? Because he first loved us! Here's how the apostle Paul described it in Ephesians 3:18–19 (emphasis mine):

> And may you have the power to understand, as all God's people should, how wide, how long, how high, and how deep his love is. May you experience the love of Christ, though it is too great to

understand fully. THEN you will be made complete with all the fullness of life and power that comes from God.

Do you see it yet? Are you beginning to understand?

I almost wish I could put fireworks and an explosion of exclamation points after that word "then" (literally translated: "to the intent that") in Ephesians 3:19.[8] But I'll spare you the punctuation fire hazard and try to explain it this way:

All of the law and prophets hang on our ability to love. We know this is true. We also know that when we experience the love of Christ, THEN we are "made complete" with "life and power that comes from God." If both those things are facts of spiritual living, then maybe it's time for us to finally admit, right now, that we are only capable of loving—and thus fulfilling all the Law and the prophets—because he first loved us.

We can understand what real love is and how to express it only if we have gratefully experienced it first from Christ. And after experiencing Jesus' stunningly generous love firsthand, the fruit of his Spirit—LOVE!—can't help but live within and through the gratefulness we feel as a result. That's when the life and power of God begin to show up in the way we live and think and act and pray and worship and serve and laugh and cry and all the other things we do.

And so I tell you again: *all* of your authentic Christian life is an expression of gratitude.

When you turn your eyes heavenward, the love you feel for the Lord your God is a *natural outflow of the gratitude his love has created in your heart*. When you level your gaze at your family, friends, neighbors, and yes, enemies—if love burns inside you toward those people, it's ignited instinctively out of uncontainable gratefulness that you *personally* have been transformed from enemy of God to child of God.

Breathe that for a moment.

Jesus loved you first. When you finally experience that transformative love, you cannot help but be grateful. When you're grateful, you can't help but generously express what you've received—and that's all it takes for you to live your Christian life.

Do you believe it?

LOVE ME DO

We love because he first loved us.

— 1 JOHN 4:19 (NIV)

Take this book with you, and go look in a nearby mirror. (If no mirror is available, go ahead and take a quick selfie and use that instead.)

Peek into the eyes that stare back at you. What do you see there? Tiredness? Pain perhaps. Laughter, maybe. Concern or worry? Curiosity, or sorrow, or hope, or something you can't quite describe. Maybe all of those things.

Now look deeper, past where the human eye can see. Beyond your appearance, what do you see when you look at yourself? Describe yourself here—your character traits, your strengths and weaknesses, your values.

Take moment to silently reread what you wrote, then read it aloud to the person in the mirror. If you've done this imagination exercise honestly, the description you wrote and read aloud is fairly close to the real you, maybe the one you hide from people at work and only show to those closest to you. Or, if you're like many, maybe you hide that person from your family and friends too, at least sometimes.

If you could talk to your mirror-self about love, what do you think Mirror-You would ask you about it? Write it here.

Some people say that we learn something of love from others, but we can only *experience* others' love to the degree with which we love ourselves.

Do you think that's true? Why or why not?

_____

_____

_____

_____

_____

_____

I'm frequently stumped by Jesus' second-greatest commandment, "Love your neighbor as yourself" (Matthew 22:39). His assumption seems to be that we already love ourselves greatly, and appropriately. But what happens when self-love is marred by self-aggrandizement or handicapped by self-loathing? Or hindered by something in between?

Truth be told, I'm very "good" at discerning how others are failing at loving themselves—and thus failing at loving me. Yet, I'm abysmal at understanding what it really means to healthily love myself, and then to healthily love others in the same way. And when I look in the mirror, I often see the failures that decorate my history instead of the person upon whom Christ has lavished his love.

"O wretched man that I am! who shall deliver me from the body of this death?" the apostle Paul wrote to Christians in Rome (Romans 7:24 KJV). Yeah, that about describes it, at least sometimes. And so when I look at my reflection and wonder what Mirror-Me would ask me about love, I think it might be something like this, "Dude, why can't you accept that it's OK to love yourself? That it's actually healthy, something good for your soul that leads you toward spiritual growth?"

The way Mirror-Me tells it, it's almost an insult to deny love to someone Christ loves. He seems to think that I'll never love others to my full potential until I can "Love my neighbor as myself."

What do you think about that?

On October 5, 1962, the Beatles released the song that would become their very first hit. Co-written by John Lennon and Paul McCartney, it was titled "Love Me Do." The song itself is simple, based on "schoolboy song scribblings" of the now-legendary McCartney.[9] This title speaks to something deep within, doesn't it? I wonder what would change within me, and outside me, and around me, if I learned to "love me" just a little bit in the way that Jesus does?

And what would change in you?

Return to that question from your conversation with Mirror-You, but now imagine that it's Jesus who is gazing back at you through your eyes. Does your question change? If so, write it here:

_____

_____

_____

_____

_____

_____

_____

"We love because he first loved us," the apostle John told us. So this is your assignment. Today, take that Scripture with you wherever you go, but try this personalization experiment with it as you live through the hours: Each time you look at a clock or watch, or check the time on your phone, say quietly to yourself, "I love myself, because he first loved me."

Use this page to journal your thoughts and prayers about what you've read today. Feel free to follow one or both of the prompts below, or to write whatever else is on your mind.

1. Go ahead and answer those two questions you wrote in today's devotion—the one Mirror-You asked, and the one Mirror-Jesus asked. Give as much explanation as you feel is necessary.

2. If you have the chance, come back here after your personalization experiment with 1 John 4:19. What happened?

DUTY AND DESIRE

We love because he first loved us.

— 1 JOHN 4:19 (NIV)

I have a friend, let's call him Solomon.

Sol's a fine young man, loves Jesus, loves his wife. He works hard, he's generous. He volunteers at church and even leads the occasional Bible study. And he really struggles with pornography.

One day Sol and I are having coffee and he shares with me his frustration with this whole temptation of watching online porn. "Why is it so hard," he asks me. "Why do I keep giving in to that when I know it's wrong, when I'm actually happy with my wife and our sex life?"

So I ask him what he's been doing about this struggle. He launches into a list of all the preventative steps he's taken, which includes (among other things) a notification app that alerts his wife every time he views porn online. I cringe. He thought this fear of being found out by his wife would be punishment enough to be a deterrent for his behavior. But of course, it wasn't.

I know Sol's wife. She's warm, pretty, talented, and loving. I can almost see the pain and shame she feels whenever that app pings on her cell phone. I can practically hear my friend's wife asking God, "Why am I not enough for Solomon? What's wrong with me?" Meanwhile I'm thinking, why should this innocent woman have to play the role of Punisher for Sol's sin? This creates a cycle of disappointment every time the app activates. It only breeds bitterness and resentment, in both husband and wife.

Sadly, my friend's struggle is a common one, because it seeks a legalistic, outward correction to an inward problem of the heart. It's the classic "appearance over substance" situation, or what Jesus might've called a "whitewashed tomb" condition (see Matthew 23:26–28).

"Why is it so hard?" Solomon asks me.

Because, I finally tell him, you've let yourself get focused on the *duty* of love instead of the *desire* of it. We love, I tell Sol, because he first loved us—because our experience with Christ motivates our expression of him. When we live the ongoing encounter described in 1 John 4:19, even the hardest obligations of love are not chores; they become cherished opportunities.

Let me tell you a story to help explain what I mean.

The last week of my wife's life she lay in a coma, unresponsive, waiting to die. I sat by her side, waiting with her, keeping a promise that she'd always have moisturizing balm on her lips, playing her favorite music softly nearby. Weeping, of course, but also holding her hand and reading to her and, well, weeping some more.

During that week, our hospice social worker stopped in to check on us regularly. He was former military, a man used to the obligations of service. He was also kind and comforting. At one point he shook his head sorrowfully and said to me, "Mike, you're a good husband. A good man." Then he stood at full attention and gave me a crisp military salute. I didn't know what to say. He shook my hand and left, and after he was gone it finally struck me:

This man thinks I'm fulfilling some husbandly duty by sitting here with Amy. He has no idea what's really going on!

You see, I wasn't sitting with Amy because it was my obligation or because it was expected of me or because it was the "right thing" to do. Heavens no! In that awful time my only desire, my only thought was that I *desperately wanted* to be nowhere else except next to her. Fulfilling my "duty" to my wife—as crushing as it was to my soul—was no chore because passion was my motivation, not obligation. All I desired was lying in that hospital bed, and so it was my blessing to be the only one whose ears heard when that beautiful soul finally breathed itself out of Amy's tiny, cancer-stained body.

So this is my point: *Desire trumps duty every time.*

And that's what I told Solomon. "Next time you're facing a pornographic temptation, don't think about what *obligates* you to turn away. Think about *what you desire more* than what tempts you."

He nodded slowly. "You mean, like knowing my wife can trust me. Seeing her smile. Knowing I don't have to feel ashamed."

Now Sol's getting it, isn't he?

"All who love me will do what I say," Jesus told his disciples at the Last Supper (John 14:23). I've heard it often preached that this statement is some kind of test for you and me. We dutifully follow God's commands first, and then that means we love Jesus, whether we are loving people or not. There could be some truth in that, but I wonder if maybe there's more to it. After all, we seem to forget that Jesus made this pronouncement while explaining an inexplicably grand promise to his disciples:

> I will ask the Father, and he will give you another Advocate, who will never leave you. *He is the Holy Spirit, who leads into all truth. . . . He will teach you everything and will remind you of everything I have told you.* —JOHN 14:16–17, 26 (emphasis mine)

When I read Jesus' statement, "All who love me will do what I say," in the context of all of John 14:15–26, I find myself wondering:

What if this is part of the promise?

What if doing what Christ says is not so much a burden that you and I must bear, but rather part of the promise that his Spirit will guide and empower us? What if Jesus was saying, at least to some extent, "When you love me, my Holy Spirit will fill you and teach and lead you so that it's natural for you to obey what I say"?

I think this might be something of what the apostle Paul meant when he wrote in Romans 8:12–13 (emphasis mine):

Therefore, dear brothers and sisters, you have no obligation to do what your sinful nature urges you to do. For if you live by its dictates, you will die. But if through the power of the Spirit you put to death the deeds of your sinful nature, you will live.

You see, duty observed without desire eventually becomes a bitter pill that causes resentment and judgment and harshness and legalism and rebellion to fester inside. But when our *desire* is for him, it seems to me, the Holy Spirit makes desire spring out of our duty to obey—something that happens naturally, unpretentiously, joyfully, lovingly . . . even passionately. Regardless of how difficult the situation, there is love and joy in obeying because Christ's Holy Spirit is in it—and those things are what he naturally builds within us (see Galatians 5:22–23).

All right, let me tell you the rest of Solomon's story. Some weeks after having coffee with my friend, I saw him again. He was practically jubilant, and reported that he'd been porn-free for months.

"Mike!" he said. "Why didn't anybody ever tell me this before? Duty and desire, so simple. When I start to struggle, I remind myself of all the great things I desire more than the temptation I'm facing—and then it's so much easier to turn away from that sin."

Duty and desire. Understanding the difference—and choosing desire as the motivation for right living—can literally change your life.

Use this page to journal your thoughts and prayers about what you've read today. Feel free to follow one or both of the prompts below, or to write whatever else is on your mind.

1. What's your initial reaction to what you read about duty and desire?

2. What duties of love would you like to change to desires? How might the Holy Spirit help you to do that? Write your answer as a letter to Christ.

THE "ENEMIES" THING

We love because he first loved us.

— 1 JOHN 4:19 (NIV)

Last week I was chatting with my granddaughter just before her bedtime. Now that my beard is long, she likes to try to braid it, or put it into a ponytail, or festoon it with red ribbons or pink hair clips or other silly things that make six-year-old girls giggle. So she was playing with my beard as we talked, and then she got a concerned look on her face.

"Dumpy," she said seriously.[10] "You know why people stop you at airports? Because your hair and beard make you look like a terror." (She meant "terrorist," but I'm just telling it to you like she told it to me.) "You should cut your beard and hair. Then people would like you and wouldn't think you're a terror."

Suddenly I found myself in an unexpected teachable moment about racism and people who unfairly see me as their enemy, simply because of the way I look.

And I had no idea what to say.

There was a moment of awkward silence between my granddaughter and me. Finally I mumbled something about how it's OK if I get stopped sometimes, and she should just go to sleep now and have happy dreams.

Yeah, I pretty much punted. But she caught me off guard.

I've been thinking about that little encounter in the days since, still wondering what I should've said. How do I help this adorable child grow into a compassionate, loving woman—who also understands this world is not frequently kind to those who are different?

See, she has a point. I am routinely stopped at airports. My clear vinyl backpack is commonly emptied, even though its see-through material reveals everything inside it at a single glance. I'm a reliable target for the TSA wand, for random chemical tests on my hands, and for the occasional pat down. I cooperate, and it's usually over quickly, but I have to admit it's sometimes frustrating to walk into an airport knowing many people there will view me with suspicion until I walk out again. Being an American of Arabic ancestry doesn't mean I deserve to be treated like an Islamic terrorist.

Of course, the airport isn't the only place where people take offense at me. Once while driving across Wyoming, I stopped for breakfast at McDonalds in Rawlins. I figured I'd take advantage of the facilities while I was there, and passed a table of four people on my way into the men's room. There were three elderly gentlemen, and one woman. They frowned at me when I walked by. When I came out, the leader of the group turned to me and said loudly, "Well

I guess now they have bathrooms for men, women, AND monkeys." His friends had a good laugh at that, and at me. What's an Arab "monkey" to do? I drove away and never looked back.

I could tell stories of being punched, spit on, and vilified with profanities. I could tell you about vandalized property, thefts, refusal of service, and more—but I think you get the idea.

Funny thing is, I was born an American. My great-grandfather earned his American citizenship more than a century ago, fighting for the United States in the trenches of World War I. My father was a sergeant in the US Army, and served during the Korean War. When he passed away (of old age), the United States government buried him with full military honors. I still have the watch he was given at the time of his honorable discharge from service. Two of my Arab-American uncles fought for America in Vietnam. But none of that matters to some people. All that matters is that I don't look like them.

And then today I read Matthew 5:44, and Jesus told me, "But I say, love your enemies! Pray for those who persecute you!"

In my mind I see those hateful people jeering at me in the venerable McDonalds of Rawlins, Wyoming. I don't want to love those old coots. I don't want to like them, or even tolerate them. I want to go back to Rawlins someday, find them still sitting in their filthy corner seats, march right up and deliver some devastatingly witty comeback—a few years too late, sure, but worth the wait. I want them to weep and apologize. After all, I wasn't the one who attacked them; they made themselves my enemies, right?

But this vengeful little fantasy is nothing more than that—a fantasy, and not a very good one. Still, it makes me wonder about my granddaughter's advice.

Would it help if I cut my hair and beard? Would people like me then? Would that make it easier for me to avoid being racially profiled or insulted or dismissed or denied something because of my ethnicity—and all the anger and hurt I feel in response? Maybe . . . but probably not. Even with short hair an Arab is still an Arab, right? So I have to go back to Jesus.

Christ told me to love my enemies, not because he knew it'd be easy, but because he knew that with his help, I could do it. See, "We love because he first loved us." That means that experiencing his love within me also empowers me to be someone who can love my enemies . . . because after all, Jesus loved me while I was his enemy. As the apostle Paul wrote, "God showed his great love for us by sending Christ to die for us while we were still sinners" (Romans 5:8).

So yes, people can be hurtful, mean, abusive, abrasive, and so much more. Of course, I don't have to stay in a situation of abuse (in fact, I shouldn't, and neither should you), but I also can't let the hatefulness of that abuse stay with me when I'm out of that situation.

When I respond with anger and plans of retaliation, I entrap myself in the abusive moment when I am actually free of it in Christ. My own emotional chains keep me bound to it, a prison of my own making. Such a waste.

The "enemies" thing is a hard teaching, because the truth is we all have enemies of one sort or another and loving them goes against human nature. That's why the solution isn't found in me, it's found instead in what Christ supernaturally does in me.

Can I love my enemies?

That depends. Can I experience the love Christ has for me?

If so, then yes, even when I don't feel like it, I can love those who oppose and denigrate me, because Christ's love for me has consequences that change the way I have love for others. And little by little, day by day, his Holy Spirit makes that difference.

NEW WORLD RECORD

We love because he first loved us.

—1 JOHN 4:19 (NIV)

Today you're going to set a new world record.

Or not. We'll see how it goes.

I want you to try to balance on one foot, without tumbling over, for at least 60 seconds. Oh, and you have to cover your eyes with your hand while you try to accomplish this New World Record.

Easy, right?

OK, whenever you're ready. Pick a spot near some form of support, like a wall, table, or counter. Stand there, close your eyes, balance on one foot, and begin counting the seconds. If you're a real pro, go ahead and set the timer on your cell phone so you don't have to count in your head.

Try it three times with your eyes closed, and write in the spaces below how many seconds you're able stay upright. Go!

World Record #1 _____

World Record #2 _____

World Record #3 _____

All right, how'd you do? Look at your "World Records" above—how many of them passed the 60 second mark?

Wait—*not a single one of your attempts* at balancing on one foot with your eyes covered reached 60 seconds? Not even 30 seconds?

Well, don't worry, Almost-World-Record-Holder, you're not alone. Unless you're a special kind of athlete, or a ballet dancer with years of training or something, your times probably all fell within the 10–20 second range. (Mine were about 12 seconds each time, though once I did hit 14 seconds. So you know, I've got that going for me.)

See, the human balance system simply isn't designed to accomplish what you just attempted. Generally speaking, people can't stand on one foot for 60 seconds with their eyes closed. So why did I make you try to do it?

Well, today I wanted you to feel just a twinge of frustration at trying to accomplish an impossible task. And I want you to remember that frustration as you try round two of our World Record Olympics.

Now, pick out an object across the room that's easily seen and stable in its position. Maybe a clock, or a picture on the wall, or your vast library of all the books written by Mike Nappa. You get the idea.

Next try the balancing act again—but this time instead of closing your eyes, focus your gaze on that object. Set the timer on your cell phone, and see how many attempts it takes before you hit 60 seconds or more of balancing on one foot.

Write your new world record in the space below.

◆ New World Record! _____

Compare your new world record with your earlier times. Pretty good, huh? If you're like most, this time you were able to hit the 60-second mark on either your first or second try. And even if you never quite got to 60 seconds, your performance still improved dramatically. So go ahead and let the theme music from the movie Rocky swell inside your head as you bask in your new triumph for a moment or two.

Feels good, doesn't it? Remember that too.

This is what's going on:

Your senses work best when they work together, so being able to use visual markers improves your physical performance. That's why ballet dancers always snap their heads back to a specific spot when performing a series of pirouettes—and why they can perform so many in a row! In fact, the simple act of balancing requires three "systems" to coordinate perfectly within you: (1) physical sensation (from your feet), (2) your inner ear, and (3) (ta-daa!) visual cues.[11] So, being able to visually focus on a stable point in the distance provides a steadying influence on the human balance system within the brain.

Here's why that's important for you to know. We've been examining day by day what love means and how to do it. As we near the end of our 29-day journey, the "now what?" question looms large. What do we do with everything we've learned? Well, at the risk of sounding a gong one too many times, the answer to "now what?" is this:

We love because he first loved us.

Listen, you'll be tempted to try to love your family, your friends, your enemies, yourself—your world—in your own strength. There'll be times when that annoying in-law will make you feel like you've got to force yourself to love, or that enemy at work will sabotage you again and you'll try to tell yourself, "Grr. Well, I have to love her, cuz that's what Jesus said to do." Your intent will be good, but your execution will fail every time.

Trying to love like Jesus takes more than you've got to give. It's like trying to balance on one foot with your eyes closed! Remember the twinge of frustration you felt when you tried to do that? Now magnify that frustration by about a million or two, and that's what happens when you try to love in your own strength, as a forced act of your will. All that does is make you feel irritated and bitter inside—and that's not love, no matter how kind you act on the outside.

So now what? When you want to love against your will, when it isn't easy, when you feel frustrated about it, remember 1 John 4:19. Pay attention to *why* you love, why you *can love* authentically in the first place. Find again the gratefulness that's intrinsic to *being loved* by Jesus—and turn to his Holy Spirit for strength to love within your unpleasant circumstances.

Now, let's not fool ourselves into thinking I am the perfect example of this principle—because I'm *not*. In fact, just this week I'm struggling to love a writer that God has placed in my care. I am trying to mentor him, teach and *help* him—and like a stiff-necked donkey he's fighting me every step of the way. So in my vanity yesterday, I insulted him personally, and even though my insult was true, it was also unnecessary and hurtful. Now my human nature wants to insult him once more as I walk out of his life with a figurative slamming of the door. But I know this is not God's intention for this man, nor for me, nor for our relationship.

So today, my prayer has been, "Lord I honestly don't want to love this guy. Help me remember how you've loved me when I was stupid and arrogant and worse—just yesterday. Have your Holy Spirit move within me so that I experience you today, and then have strength to share that experience with him tomorrow." What my thick-headed, egotistical brain is slowly learning as I pray through this situation is this:

Jesus Christ honestly will help you love others (and yourself) in any circumstance, through any day. He *can and will* create that kind of love-triumph within you—but you've got to let God do the heavy lifting instead of straining to do it all by yourself.

You want to love better horizontally, sharing Christ's love easily with those around you? Then train yourself to start every relationship moment vertically—looking gratefully to

God first, last, and every minute in between.

Hey, maybe you'll set a new world record.

U se this page to journal your thoughts and prayers about what you've read today. Feel free to follow one or both of the prompts below, or to write whatever else is on your mind.

1. "We love because he first loved us." In your daily life, what do you think it looks like to love others as a response to God's love for you? Make a list.

2. Next time you're finding it difficult to love sincerely in both your thoughts and actions, what kind of prayer would you like to pray to ask for help? Write a model of that prayer here.

TTFN

We love because he first loved us.

—1 JOHN 4:19 (NIV)

I f you've ever seen the 1968 Walt Disney classic film, *Winnie the Pooh and the Blustery Day*, then you know the phrase "TTFN." Spoken by the bouncy, trouncy, flouncy, pouncy, fun-fun-fun-fun-fun Tigger, it means "Ta Ta For Now"—his exit sentiment to the puzzled Pooh-Bear watching him leave.[12]

Today is the last of our four "outside of our comfort zone," days, our final day together to stretch our boundaries and get beyond our isolated little bubbles. So in the spirit of good ol' Tigger, I've got four goals for you to accomplish, and they can also be summed up as "TTFN."

I. THANK SOMEONE FOR LOVING YOU

Make this personal, and meaningful. Think of one person whose love has changed you, whose selfless care has helped build you into who you are today. If possible, I'd encourage you to choose someone outside your immediate family—just to stretch yourself a bit. Then create a specific, memorable way to say "Thank You" to that person. You can write a letter, or draw a picture, or put together a scrapbook, or mow it in the lawn, or write a song, or whatever your creative mind can think of. But plan to do this before the end of the day (you can start this tomorrow morning if necessary), and make sure the person you choose knows without a doubt how grateful you are to be the recipient of their love.

2. TELL SOMEONE YOU LOVE THEM

Again, make this personal and meaningful. And I'd encourage you to choose someone outside your immediate family. Make time stop somehow, and in that moment where there's nothing but you and the one you love, be very clear and determined about expressing your love to this person. Pretend it's the last chance you'll ever have to say what you truly feel about that person. And then, you know, write a letter, or draw a picture, or put together a scrapbook, or mow it in the lawn, or write a song, or whatever your creative mind can think of.

3. FIND SOMEONE NEW TO LOVE

It can be difficult at times to reach beyond our boundaries and love outside of our comfort zone. It can also be one of the more rewarding experiences of the human life. So spend some time today praying and thinking about someone new that you'd like to be intentional about loving in the next year. Maybe it's a neighbor, or a coworker, or someone at your church, or a child in Malawi, or a grumpy old man with a white beard down to his clavicle, or whomever God points your heart toward. After you've chosen the right person, begin brainstorming ways to build that relationship and express love toward him or her. Try to come up with a list of 12 possible ways to begin expressing love to that person in the coming year.

4. NETWORK WITH MIKE

OK, this one's actually optional, but I hope you'll do it anyway. Sometime before you nod off to sleep tonight, maybe you'll send me an email, just to tell me about your experience with this book. You can tell me anything—good or bad—because just hearing from you will let me know that you read this, that you took time to think about it, and that maybe you did the unusual challenges we undertook together to learn to love better in only 29 days. To me, that's an expression of love I'll cherish.

You can reach me anytime on LinkedIn or Facebook, or at this email address: bookclub@nappaland.com.

TTFN!

THE MOST
IMPORTANT PARTS

IF YOU DON'T READ ANYTHING ELSE . . .

But the Holy Spirit produces this kind of fruit in our lives: love, joy, peace, patience, kindness, goodness, faithfulness, gentleness, and self-control. There is no law against these things!
—GALATIANS 5:22–23

All of us, like sheep, have strayed away. We have left God's paths to follow our own. —ISAIAH 53:6

The LORD looks down from heaven on the entire human race; he looks to see if anyone is truly wise, if anyone seeks God. But no, all have turned away; all have become corrupt. No one does good, not a single one! —PSALM 14:2–3

For the sinful nature is always hostile to God. It never did obey God's laws, and it never will. That's why those who are still under the control of their sinful nature can never please God. —ROMANS 8:7–8

"Everyone who sins is a slave of sin." —JOHN 8:34

For everyone has sinned; we all fall short of God's glorious standard. —ROMANS 3:23

"Remain in me, and I will remain in you. For a branch cannot produce fruit if it is severed from the vine, and you cannot be fruitful unless you remain in me. Yes, I am the vine; you are the branches. Those who remain in me, and I in them, will produce much fruit. For apart from me you can do nothing." —JOHN 15:4–5

"Anyone who has seen me has seen the Father!" —JOHN 14:9

"Don't misunderstand why I have come. I did not come to abolish the law of Moses or the writings of the prophets. No, I came to accomplish their purpose." —MATTHEW 5:17

Mercy and truth are met together; righteousness and peace have kissed each other. —PSALM 85:10 (KJV)

Jesus returned to the Mount of Olives, but early the next morning he was back again at the Temple. A crowd soon gathered, and he sat down and taught them. As he was speaking, the teachers of religious law and the Pharisees brought a woman who had been caught in the act of adultery. They put her in front of the crowd.

"Teacher," they said to Jesus, "this woman was caught in the act of adultery. The law of Moses says to stone her. What do you say?"

They were trying to trap him into saying something they could use against him, but Jesus stooped down and wrote in the dust with his finger. They kept demanding an answer, so he stood up again and said, "All right, but let the one who has never sinned throw the first stone!" Then he stooped down again and wrote in the dust.

When the accusers heard this, they slipped away one by one, beginning with the oldest, until only Jesus was left in the middle of the crowd with the woman. Then Jesus stood up again and said to the woman, "Where are your accusers? Didn't even one of them condemn you?"

"No, Lord," she said.

And Jesus said, "Neither do I. Go and sin no more."
—JOHN 8:1–11

God is love. —1 JOHN 4:8

＊

Now we see things imperfectly, like puzzling reflections in a mirror. —1 CORINTHIANS 13:12

＊

"Come to me, all of you who are weary and carry heavy burdens." —MATTHEW 11:28

＊

"I tell you, her sins—and they are many—have been forgiven, so she has shown me much love. But a person who is forgiven little shows only little love." —LUKE 7:47

＊

See how very much our Father loves us, for he calls us his children, and that is what we are! —1 JOHN 3:1

＊

We know what real love is because Jesus gave up his life for us. —1 JOHN 3:16

＊

And this hope will not lead to disappointment. For we know how dearly God loves us, because he has given us the Holy Spirit to fill our hearts with his love. —ROMANS 5:5

And I am convinced that nothing can ever separate us from God's love. Neither death nor life, neither angels nor demons, neither our fears for today nor our worries about tomorrow—not even the powers of hell can separate us from God's love. No power in the sky above or in the earth below—indeed, nothing in all creation will ever be able to separate us from the love of God that is revealed in Christ Jesus our Lord. —ROMANS 8:38–39

Bring Mark with you when you come, for he will be helpful to me in my ministry. —2 TIMOTHY 4:11

"The Father and I are one." —JOHN 10:30

Love is patient, love is kind. It does not envy, it does not boast, it is not proud. It does not dishonor others, it is not self-seeking, it is not easily angered, it keeps no record of wrongs. Love does not delight in evil but rejoices with the truth. It always protects, always trusts, always hopes, always perseveres. Love never fails. —1 CORINTHIANS 13:4–8 (NIV)

We have peace with God because of what Jesus Christ our Lord has done for us. —ROMANS 5:1

But to all who believed him and accepted him,
he gave the right to become children of God.
—JOHN 1:12

And because we are his children, God has sent the
Spirit of his Son into our hearts, prompting us to
call out, "Abba, Father." —GALATIANS 4:6

After some time Paul said to Barnabas, "Let's
go back and visit each city where we previously
preached the word of the Lord, to see how the new
believers are doing." Barnabas agreed and wanted
to take along John Mark. But Paul disagreed
strongly, since John Mark had deserted them in
Pamphylia and had not continued with them in their
work. Their disagreement was so sharp that they
separated. Barnabas took John Mark with him and
sailed for Cyprus. Paul chose Silas, and as he left,
the believers entrusted him to the Lord's gracious
care. —ACTS 15:36–40

When I look at the night sky and see the work of
your fingers—the moon and the stars you set in
place—what are mere mortals that you should think
about them, human beings that you should care for
them? —PSALM 8:3–4

For we are God's masterpiece. He has created us anew in Christ Jesus, so we can do the good things he planned for us long ago. —EPHESIANS 2:10

You are a chosen people. You are royal priests, a holy nation, God's very own possession.
—1 PETER 2:9

And I am certain that God, who began the good work within you, will continue his work until it is finally finished on the day when Christ Jesus returns. —PHILIPPIANS 1:6

Let me hear of your unfailing love each morning, for I am trusting you. Show me where to walk, for I give myself to you. —PSALM 143:8

To illustrate the point further, Jesus told them this story: "A man had two sons. The younger son told his father, 'I want my share of your estate now before you die.' So his father agreed to divide his wealth between his sons.

"A few days later this younger son packed all his belongings and moved to a distant land, and there he wasted all his money in wild living. About the time his money ran out, a great famine swept over the land, and he began to starve. He persuaded a local farmer to hire him, and the man sent him into his fields to feed the pigs. The young man became so hungry that even the pods he was feeding the pigs looked good to him. But no one gave him anything.

"When he finally came to his senses, he said to himself, 'At home even the hired servants have food enough to spare, and here I am dying of hunger! I will go home to my father and say, "Father, I have sinned against both heaven and you, and I am no longer worthy of being called your son. Please take me on as a hired servant."'

"So he returned home to his father. And while he was still a long way off, his father saw him coming. Filled with love and compassion, he ran to his son, embraced him, and kissed him. His son said to him, 'Father, I have sinned against both heaven and you, and I am no longer worthy of being called your son.'

"But his father said to the servants, 'Quick! Bring the finest robe in the house and put it on him. Get a ring for his finger and sandals for his feet. And kill the calf we have been fattening. We must celebrate with a feast, for this son of mine was dead and has now returned to life. He was lost, but now he is found.' So the party began.

"Meanwhile, the older son was in the fields working. When he returned home, he heard music and dancing in the house, and he asked one of the servants what was going on. 'Your brother is back,' he was told, 'and your father has killed the fattened calf. We are celebrating because of his safe return.'

"The older brother was angry and wouldn't go in. His father came out and begged him, but he replied, 'All these years I've slaved for you and never once refused to do a single thing you told me to. And in all that time you never gave me even one young goat for a feast with my friends. Yet when this son of yours comes back after squandering your money on prostitutes, you celebrate by killing the fattened calf!'

"His father said to him, 'Look, dear son, you have always stayed by me, and everything I have is yours. We had to celebrate this happy day. For your brother was dead and has come back to life! He was lost, but now he is found!'" —LUKE 15:11–32

❧

"Dear brothers and sisters, when I was with you I couldn't talk to you as I would to spiritual people. I had to talk . . . as though you were infants in Christ. I had to feed you with milk, not with solid food, because you weren't ready for anything stronger.
—1 CORINTHIANS 3:1–2

And may you have the power to understand, as all God's people should, how wide, how long, how high, and how deep his love is. May you experience the love of Christ, though it is too great to understand fully. Then you will be made complete with all the fullness of life and power that comes from God. —EPHESIANS 3:18–19

But I say, love your enemies! Pray for those who persecute you! —MATTHEW 5:44

Therefore, dear brothers and sisters, you have no obligation to do what your sinful nature urges you to do. For if you live by its dictates, you will die. But if through the power of the Spirit you put to death the deeds of your sinful nature, you will live.
—ROMANS 8:12–13

"If you love me, obey my commandments. And I will ask the Father, and he will give you another Advocate, who will never leave you. He is the Holy Spirit, who leads into all truth. The world cannot receive him, because it isn't looking for him and doesn't recognize him. But you know him, because he lives with you now and later will be in you. No, I will not abandon you as orphans—I will come to you. Soon the world will no longer see me, but you will see me. Since I live, you also will live. When I am raised to life again, you will know that I am in my Father, and you are in me, and I am in you. Those who accept my commandments and obey them are the ones who love me. And because they love me, my Father will love them. And I will love them and reveal myself to each of them."

Judas (not Judas Iscariot, but the other disciple with that name) said to him, "Lord, why are you going to reveal yourself only to us and not to the world at large?"

Jesus replied, "All who love me will do what I say. My Father will love them, and we will come and make our home with each of them. Anyone who doesn't love me will not obey me. And remember, my words are not my own. What I am telling you is from the Father who sent me. I am telling you these things now while I am still with you. But when the Father sends the Advocate as my representative— that is, the Holy Spirit—he will teach you everything and will remind you of everything I have told you."
—JOHN 14:15–26

O wretched man that I am! who shall deliver me from the body of this death? —ROMANS 7:24 (KJV)

We love because he first loved us. —1 JOHN 4:19 (NIV)

One of them, an expert in the law, tested him with this question: "Teacher, which is the greatest commandment in the Law [of Moses]?" Jesus replied: "'Love the Lord your God with all your heart and with all your soul and with all your mind.' This is the first and greatest commandment. And the second is like it: 'Love your neighbor as yourself.' All the Law and the Prophets hang on these two commandments." —MATTHEW 22:35–40 (NIV)

NOTES

1 Bruce Olson, *Bruchko* (Orlando, FL: Charisma House, 1978), 133.

2 "Bridge Collapses in Atlanta Freeway Fire During Rush Hour," *NBC News*, March 31, 2017, https://www.nbcnews.com/news/us-news/bridge-collapses-atlanta-freeway-fire-during-rush-hour-n740871.

3 "Burn one's bridges and burn one's boats," *Grammarist*, accessed January 23, 2019, https://grammarist.com/idiom/burn-ones-bridges-and-burn-ones-boats/.

4 Clinton E. Arnold, ed. *Zondervan Illustrated Bible Backgrounds Commentary*, vol. 1 (Grand Rapids: Zondervan, 2002), 447.

5 Tremper Longman III, ed. *The Baker Illustrated Bible Dictionary* (Grand Rapids: Baker Books, 2013), 1361.

6 Rick Reilly, "In Like Flynn," *Sports Illustrated*. February 11, 2002, 108. Filip Bondy, "Meet Dion Rich, the notorious Super Bowl gatecrasher who has set his sights on NY," *New York Daily News* online. January 25, 2014. Accessed May 14, 2019. https://www.nydailynews.com/sports/football/bondy-meet-notorious-super-bowl-crasher-set-sights-ny-article-1.1591379.

7 Charles R. Swindoll, *Swindoll's New Testament Insights: Insights on Romans* (Grand Rapids: Zondervan, 2010), 118.

8 Joseph H. Thayer, *Thayer's Greek-English Lexicon of the New Testament* (Grand Rapids: Baker Books, 1977), 302.

9 Jack Doyle, "Love Me Do: 1962-2012," PopHistoryDig.com, October 7, 2012.

10 Yes, my granddaughter calls me "Dumpy." There's story behind it, but I won't bore you with that here. Just suffice it to say, that's what she calls me and I like it.

11 Young Choi, "Why Do I Lose Balance When I Close My Eyes?," *Healthtap*, Accessed June 01, 2019, https://www.healthtap.com/user_questions/935908-why-do-i-lose-balane-when-i-close-my-eyes.

12 Paul Winchell (as Tigger). *Winnie the Pooh and the Blustery Day*, directed by Wolfgang Reitherman (Burbank, CA: Walt Disney), 1968.